D0574383

Spirit Animals

By Victoria Covell
Illustrations by Noah Buchanan

DAWN PUBLICATIONS

To the gifted man who read the wind on the water,
and the vibrant woman who nightly roamed the cliffs to talk to the owls,
and to their eternal love,
we dedicate this book,
with all a daughter's and a grandson's love.
—VC & NB

Copyright ©2000 Victoria Covell
Illustrations copyright ©2000 Noah Buchanan

Library of Congress Cataloging-in-Publication Data

Covell, Victoria, 1951-
  Spirit animals / by Victoria Covell ; illustrations by Noah Buchanan.
    p. cm.
ISBN 1-58469-010-0
 1. Animals—Religious aspects. 2. Spiritual life. I. Title.
 BL439 .C68 2000
 291.2'12—dc21
                              00-008828

Printed in Hong Kong

Published by Dawn Publications
P.O. Box 2010
Nevada City, CA 95959
(530) 478-0111

10 9 8 7 6 5 4 3 2 1

Design & Computer production by Andrea Miles

*W*e need another and a wiser and perhaps a more mystical concept of animals. . . . We patronize them for their incompleteness, for their tragic fate of having taken form so far below ourselves. And therein we err, and greatly err. For the animal shall not be measured by man. In a world older and more complete than ours, they move finished and completed, gifted with extensions of the senses we have lost or never attained, living by voices we shall never hear. They are not brethren, they are not underlings; they are other nations, caught with ourselves in the net of life and time, fellow prisoners of the splendor and travail of the earth.

—Henry Beston (1888-1968),
The Outermost House

Contents

A Note from the Author

ature heals us if we allow it, elevates us if we believe in it, and brings us into the sacred experience if we honor it. A relationship with the fellow species of Earth is a powerful path of self-knowledge and healing.

Have you ever had an encounter with a wild animal in which it looked straight into your eyes, as if it were trying to give you a message? That is exactly what was happening! Wild animals come to honor you with the generous gift of themselves. Obeying a prompting from our common Creator, Spirit Animals let themselves be seen either in the natural world or in your dreams or visions, in order to deliver an important message. Sometimes their message is practical and pertinent; sometimes it is a prompting to remember the primal knowledge of the heart. It might be honoring an existing strength you possess or warning of a weakness you need to challenge. It might concern a change you need to make or something precious you need to find within. It might be a vision of what you could become or a warning of what you do not want to become. Spirit Animals often come to give you the opportunity to understand the world and your role in it, or to show you a pathway through uncertain or difficult terrain.

If you are quiet enough within, many powerful insights into yourself and your journey here on Earth can be taught by animals. *Spirit Animals* is a guide to help develop a deeper intuitive relationship and communication with animals, in both their physical and subtle spirit forms. If you need an answer to a question, by opening this book with intuitive intent, *Spirit Animals* becomes a window into a mystical dimension.

Throughout human civilization, especially in pre-materialist times, animals have spoken powerfully to the human psyche and our need for the sacred experience. Many indigenous peoples all over the Earth, as well as naturalists, have long believed in the power of animals to bring messages, to create beauty, and to inspire or enhance the human experience. For example, Australian aborigines have long held that in the beginning of all time—in Dreamtime—the ancestors of all living beings were animal-like beings such as the hare-wallaby, the kangaroo, and the snake. They believe that all men were descended from these ancestors and are therefore bound together as one with all creatures. Native Americans have sacred creation myths in which animals such as the bison, the turtle, and the raven are honored as representing the Creator. They also believe that wild animals appear in our lives to bring us messages of self-awareness, encouragement, recognition, and warning. Today many people feel their mythic roots when following the "spirit footsteps" of Native Americans. These "spiritual naturalists" who value creation as the endowment of the Creator, believe in the inherent ability of all creation to teach, inspire, and be an intimate part of one's life. For these spiritual naturalists who live life as a vision quest, looking for the raw moment of self-awareness and self-transformation, animals are gifted partners.

The Meaning of Wild Animal Encounters

Not every encounter with another species necessarily contains within it a personal message. Birds hopping around your birdfeeder; wasps hovering by your barn door; or bears meandering into your campsite in Yosemite, might not contain a deliberate and spiritual message meant just for you. (Although depending on the circumstances, they might.) Ultimately, the meaning you make of it is left up to your own viewpoint. An experience that appears to one person as merely an interesting mystery, would to another be authentic and relevant life information, or even to another a sacred initiation into a visionary path. Many naturalists and animal enthusiasts are fulfilled by merely witnessing a species' native beauty, enjoying it for its intrinsic worth alone. For instance, wildlife biologists, intimately devoted to research, often achieve great passion in attaining in-depth awareness of a single species. They have no need or desire to apply the experience to themselves or to develop a deeper spiritual relationship with that animal.

But there are others who sense that there may be a deeper personal or mystical meaning. I am often asked by people after they have had a wild animal encounter, "What did that mean?" *Spirit Animals* offers possible messages that wild animals may bring you, focusing on the special qualities that each animal particularly embodies. These suggestions are to aid your own intuition in sensing the right meaning for you.

So how does one know when an encounter is personally symbolic? When is an experience infused with a compelling message and when is it just a special, yet normal event? Often it is the highly unusual nature of the encounter; or an animal's uncharacteristic or intimate behavior, or perhaps a too unbelievable "coincidence." It may be a special moment, charged with energy that prompts your intuition. Sometimes it is as simple as the recognition that you have crossed an unseen threshold from the ordinary into the extraordinary. To a young girl sitting on the beach, grieving the recent death of her mother, a whale displaying a full breach in front of her was powerfully personal. To a man camping alone in the woods, seeing seven geese flying repeatedly in a perfect circle directly over his head was a moving and intense omen. To a professional bird carver struggling with an accurate representation of a dove, a real dove that flew into his studio and landed in front of him on his carving table was spiritually stunning. The dove appeared just when he needed help, stayed for the several days it took to complete the carving, and then flew away and never returned. These are examples of transforming encounters with Spirit Animals which happen daily to people everywhere.

Healing Our Earth Community

Learning the soul language of Spirit Animals is a powerful tool to assist the healing of our Earth community as well. "Gifting" yourself to another species, through an "ecology of heart," fortifies the integrity of the diverse community of Earth. Each time you have a wild animal encounter, you strengthen the mystic bond between our species and theirs, thus spiritually reinforcing the entire Earth community. Spirit Animals are threads that connect our core wildness with our inherent divinity. If, like spider mother, you weave each intentional act with honor and love, you strengthen the connecting threads of all life within the web, so that all may continue to live safely and prosper in beauty. For as you increase your understanding of any other being, your respect for all creation increases, motivating compassionate, protective action. By engaging in this vital work of preserving diversity and wildness, you help ensure a sustainable planetary community in alliance with all of Earth's inhabitants.

In choosing to have a relationship with Spirit Animals, you make the decision to supplement the material dimension with a mystical one. This momentous decision of the heart delivers both life-transforming trials and generous revelations. This choice requires you to walk the trail on the knife's cutting edge. While not a path of comfort, it is one that will birth you into a vividly gifted life. Welcome to a unique world, where dwelling under the Great Spirit's sky, all creatures are universal relations. Welcome to the sacred world of Spirit Animals.

Victoria Covell
Nevada City, California
May, 2000

n the beginning of all things, wisdom and knowledge were with the animals; for Tirawa, the One Above, did not speak directly to man. He sent certain animals to tell men that He showed Himself through beasts, and that from them, and from the stars and the sun and the moon, man should learn. Tirawa spoke to man through His works...all things speak of Tirawa.

—Letakots-Lesa, Chief of the Pawnee

Badger

The Warrior Who Speaks The Truth

If Badger has chosen to appear to you, it is asking you to encourage that part of yourself that vigorously stands up for what you believe in.

The warrior Badger spirit is willing to fight to uphold the integrity of its beliefs. Even if in the minority, Badger is resolved never to back down. The hallmark of Badger is its determination and persistence. It ferociously digs to the roots of truth. It never lets falsehood remain concealed, however deep it may be hidden. Badger is not impeded by obstacles when it sees a potential beyond. If you have encountered Badger, it is time to stand up to someone or something in your life that is not in integrity. Use the Badger warrior spirit. Speak your truth.

BEWARE of attacking an individual when the real enemy is their erroneous belief.

9

The Defiant Badger

MALHEUR NATIONAL WILDLIFE REFUGE in Oregon is the largest fresh water marsh in western United States and a rich oasis for wildlife in the desert. On one of my visits a wildlife photographer was also there, photographing a pair of trumpeter swans who were elegantly floating amidst the cattails in a pond, with their little cygnets trailing behind them. He had, by chance, discovered a badger den and was watching it through the telephoto lens of his camera. There, much to our excitement, were three little badger cubs rambunctiously playing and flopping around on the apron of the den. Wrestling and tumbling, they were playing "tag" just as human children do—having a great time while Mom was out hunting. We watched, spellbound, for hours. It reminded me of a special encounter I had with a badger, when I was a young man.

I was attending a science camp in central Oregon, in countryside of sagebrush, rocky ravines, steep cliffs, and sharp switchbacks on hilly roads. One day on my way back to camp, I was driving slowly up a winding road, when a badger suddenly appeared on the side of the road. She dashed across the road in front of the car, carrying a headless jackrabbit in her mouth. I brought the car to a stop and watched her as she climbed the hill next to the car. Half way up she stopped and turned to look back, fiercely glaring down at me—ready to do battle if necessary, challenging me, a human many times her size, in case I had a notion to take her rabbit. In that brief but intense moment of contact, I was struck by her fierce, dense energy. It felt like all the intense energy of a wolf compacted into an animal the size of a house cat. In that timeless connection, we locked eyes and it seemed I could see all the way into her soul, and she into mine. When she turned and ran into the underbrush with her rabbit, the spell was broken, and I drove back to camp shaking my head in complete wonder.

Later that year, on a bitterly cold winter day in December, I was driving that same stretch of road. I spotted something lying dead on the road and I stopped to check it out. My heart sank—it was a badger. Could it possibly be my fiercely defiant badger, now lying here so still and frozen? Months earlier I had powerfully experienced its intense living energy, and now here I was holding it quietly in my hands. Examining her incredibly strong, turgid muscles and long, long claws that were cupped like spoons for spatula-like digging, I could still feel her amazing power. I stayed there for a long time to honor her and her beauty.

These memories accompanied me as I looked beyond the swans in the wildlife preserve, at these beautiful, playful badger pups. It was hard to believe that they too, would one day become fierce and warrior-like hunters, just like the determined animal on the road, a proud badger with a prize rabbit, who would never—no matter what—let go.

—David Lukas.

David Lukas is a naturalist living in the Sierra Nevada foothills. He is a nature writer whose work has appeared in magazines such as Audubon, Orion, Wild Bird, and California Wild. He is the author of "Watchable Birds of the Great Basin," Mountain Press (1999).

—Badger Facts

The ferocious badger, a member of the weasel family, is known for its incredible digging abilities. It can out-dig any other mammal, including a man with a shovel! There are even stories of badgers digging holes into pavement or concrete two inches thick! It has a fearless "never say die" attitude. Its tremendous courage, powerful muscles, fast reflexes and sharp two inch long claws allow it to hold off and even defeat an entire pack of dogs, killing animals four times its size. In the Snake River Canyon of Idaho, badgers have been seen killing and eating rattlesnakes. When its main predators— men, bears, wolves or mountain lions—attack, the badger may hold its own, or if necessary, burrow its way to safety. After shoveling dirt into the face of its attackers, the badger will disappear within minutes. The Aztecs Indians called the badger "talcoyote" or "coyote of the Earth." Formerly plentiful across western North America, the badger is now rarely seen.

BEAR

The Courage To Live With An Open Heart

If Bear has chosen to appear to you, it is asking you to encourage that part of yourself that lives from the strength of a powerful heart.

Bear spirit takes power from a heart of great capacity—strengthened and motivated by love—to stand up to aggression. It refuses, even out of self-protection, to shut its heart to another. Bear understands that only that which is accomplished with love has lasting value. It fearlessly and courageously clears away the blocks to progress. Bear spirit is a powerful teacher in sensing when to cling to your innate wildness and when to yield or adapt, and how to maintain the balance between them. If you have encountered the spirit of Bear, you will use your powerful heart to forgive and bless those you have encountered on the path already traveled, thus creating healing for the path ahead. You now become a Bear-hearted peacemaker.

REMEMBER that love blazes a far wider path than the repelling force of anger ever could.

13

Dancing with Bears

OMING FROM A TWO-WEEK expedition leading a group into the Arctic wilderness, I decided to take a quick solo trip to Denali in Alaska. Before I left, a good friend of mine who is a Navajo healer heard that I was going into grizzly bear country. He suggested I take an offering with me to "introduce-myself" to the bears. We made a powdered offering that I put in a small pouch, intending to place it, with honor, in the track of a bear. Although I had seen a lot of evidence of bears in the Arctic tundra, it was during this trip to the glaciers of Denali that I had one of the greatest encounters I have ever had with a bear, or any animal for that matter.

When I arrived in Denali I could see bears everywhere, traveling slowly across the tundra. You couldn't miss their big piles of scat, filled with berries. "What am I doing here, alone amidst all these grizzlies?" I asked myself. After several days of climbing, I decided to spend my last night camped in a cottonwood grove, resplendent in fall colors, at the base of the glaciers. I had seen plenty of bears around that day. "Tonight's the night!" I thought. I headed to a dry creek bed. I thought I heard something, but I wasn't sure. Then 100 yards down the creek I saw the biggest bear track I'd ever seen. A perfect print in the mud—I could see each claw distinctly—and it was fresh, very fresh, maybe laid down only an hour or two earlier. So I thought, "This is it, the sun is going down, it's my last chance to honor this beautiful creature, the spirit of Alaska."

I sat down and took out my pouch. As I placed my offering within the track, I sang some songs my Navajo friend had taught me. I could truly feel the spirit of the land and the bears, which felt to me to be the main spirits of this wild place. I said some prayers in reverence and appreciation for the bear, to simply say "thank you." Moments later, there was a gigantic rustle in the brush next to me. I looked up to see the biggest bear I had ever seen, standing eight feet high on his hind legs, not more than 20 yards from me! As a practiced tracker, I had entered his area stealthily and down wind. He had neither heard me nor smelled me. We had surprised each other! Every hair on my neck went up. My skin was covered in goose bumps. I froze as I waited to see what he would do next. Would he drop down and show me his side, a sign of warning? Would he paw the ground in anger and then . . .? I realized we were so close that I could hear his breathing!

We looked deeply into each other's eyes for what seemed like eternity. Much to my relief he began calmly to continue his berry foraging. I felt no threat, and very slowly I backed off. He shuffled a little in my direction, eating berries. I backed off some more. Again he moved in my direction. As he moved forward, I backed up; when I stopped, he stopped, over and over, in a slow shuffling dance! As I observed him, I kept thinking to myself how this was going to change my life, and my whole sense of animals in

general. It was the most intimate contact I have ever had, before or since, with a wild animal. I was no longer watching the bear outside of myself; he had moved inside of me and we were a part of each other. The last I saw of him was a flash of silver fur in the fading light as he crossed the glacier. I hardly slept that night, I was so thoroughly moved.

Only a few hours later, I was stunned to find myself on a flight back to San Francisco. Back in my apartment, it was hard to adjust to the confinement of modern city life. I awoke in the middle of the night, not knowing where I was, but listening for bears. I looked around me at the stifling walls of my room. Tears came down my face. Lying on my soft bed, I realized the wildness was gone. Somewhere, very far away, a single bear was crossing a glacier in the moonlight. And I? I moved with him, in a dance.

—Michael Eller

Michael is a professional wilderness guide, leading individuals, families, businesses and groups on transformational journeys and wilderness retreats throughout the world since 1972. He is the founder and director of First Light Journeys, 3594 Burnside Rd., Sebastopol, California 95472 (MCEller@ microweb.com)

—Bear Facts

Many Native American tribes believe the bear to be a deity. When Europeans first arrived in North America, brown bears ranged over most of the western part of the continent; it is estimated that there were 50,000 to 100,000 grizzlies in the American West. Yet, like the wolf, the grizzly was gunned to near-extinction by early settlers. Today, fewer than 1,000 grizzlies live south of Canada, mainly in the national parks of Montana, Wyoming, and Idaho. Grizzly bears need huge wilderness areas, many hundreds or even thousands of square miles to roam. It is believed that the population of tens of thousands of grizzly bears in Alaska and Canada is greatly declining due to vast clear-cut logging operations in their territories. Grizzly bears are one of the slowest reproducing mammals in North America.

Bee

Service for the Good of All

If *Bee* has chosen to appear to you, it is asking you to encourage that part of yourself that actively and unselfishly works for the good of others.

Never daunted, Bee spirit is lively and is agreeable to teamwork. Not afraid of hard work, Bee learns new tasks, always willing to do more than its part. Bee is not primarily focused on personal goals, but strives, with the help of others, to achieve a common goal of balance and harmony for the whole community. It holds itself accountable for the cohesive success of the whole. An encounter with Bee spirit encourages you to arouse your serviceful nature, understanding that the joy and sweetness of life is found, not in self-service, but in concentrated service to the larger community.

BEWARE of getting so caught up in habitual duties that you forget to see spontaneous beauty appearing everywhere.

The Bee Man of Pine Island

LL THE TIME I WAS growing up, one thing I always did every summer was to save bees. I'm sure my friends and family thought I was very odd, but I could never bear to watch them drown in the pond or the creek in our woods. As their self-appointed savior, I would always gather them—a sodden lump, barely alive —and place them on a dry hot rock. Then I would closely watch the magic begin. Slowly they would stir to life, pull out one tiny leg at a time and begin the slow business of grooming their little bodies. Each antennae would pop up and finally their see-through wings. Soon, they would be dry and alert, and fly away. Sometimes I would have so many on the mend that I felt as though I was running a busy emergency room at an insect hospital. I used to believe that some day, when I arrived in heaven, there would be hundreds of little bee souls that I had saved, giving testimony in my behalf. I believed the Queen of All Bees would be there to commend me and honor me in a special ceremony.

Little did I know that this behavior would be passed down to my youngest son. We lived on a tropical jungle island in the Gulf, teeming with insects, including bees. At the very early age of four he began to follow my tradition of saving drowning bees. He saved them from oceans, ponds, sudden pools of tropical downpours, and even the community swimming pool. He quickly got the attention of everyone on the island that saw him do this. As they watched him paddling around in the water, with his fingers upraised with sodden insects, they would ask me in astonishment: "What is your little boy doing?" And I would calmly respond, with a smile, "He's saving the bees."

It wasn't at all unusual to see him pedaling furiously down the street on his bike with the training wheels, with a bee on an upraised finger, and maybe a dragonfly or two on another. He would arrive into my arms with great concern because one of the little victims would not be responding. He took my care of the bees to a new level. He loved each and every one with a tender heart that would even cause him to cry if any of them died. People on the island took to calling him "the Bee Man" and pointing him out to others. I would often hear his story being told by someone, to anyone else who would listen. Sometimes people would come up to me in subtle reproach and ask me if I wasn't worried that my baby would be stung. I would always reply, "No, he never will be stung." And he never was.

To tell the truth, even today, as a grown woman, I still think the bees will defend me to St. Peter when I arrive in heaven—that is, if they're not too busy asking me what the Bee Man is up to. —V.C.

—Bee Facts

Bees are often described as social creatures, but they are more than that, they are actually communal. Every member has a particular job. Through their group efforts they put up food for winter, generally much more than they will ever need; but if the winter is long and difficult, and the honey supply runs short, they continue to share equally. Accordingly, a whole hive may starve simultaneously. Never are some of its members ejected so that others might live. Bees are also famous for sharing information by a unique method of sign language. When a bee returns to its hive with pollen found from a new source, it performs a special dance ritual to share information with other members of its hive. While the other bees stand by, observing closely, the returning bee delivers a message that accurately describes the kind, distance and exact direction of the new source of pollen. She does this by "dancing" in special circular movements. Round dances mean the pollen is nearby and tail-wagging wriggles mean it is distant. The speed with which she makes the circles denotes the distance to the pollen. (Nine circles in fifteen seconds show it to be less than 100 yards from the hive, while two circles in fifteen seconds describe it to be a mile away.) The movements are also positioned to show the relationship of the pollen in degrees to the current position of the sun. (A straight line means directly toward the sun.) By regurgitating a bit of the new pollen, the others know what species of plant they are searching for, and by the creative dance, they know just where to find it.

Bison

Holding Sacred
The Ancient Wisdom

If **Bison** has chosen to appear to you, it is
asking you to encourage that part of yourself that
connects you to universal wisdom.

*B ison spirit is the cohesive intelligence that connects
every being in creation to the wisdom that is encoded
within it, regardless of size or species. Bison spirit is
the thought-image of the Creator that is equally imprinted on
the heart of every being. Wisdom is an active force that spans
the vast ground space of the universe, from infinitesimal quarks
to infinite galaxies. When you encounter Bison spirit, your
wisdom nature is calling you to awaken to a sacred code within,
to move forward and claim your unique part in the hoop of life.
Do not be afraid to honor your own power. All the
discriminating wisdom you require will be found from the
Infinite Source, reflected in the pool of your own heart.*

**BEWARE of the greedy or arrogant use of
intelligence that selfishly slaughters conscience on
the plains of your humanity.**

In Their Midst

HAT WERE THOSE DARK shapes covering the river valley floor below? It was still too dark and misty to see well. Was it a small herd of buffalo? My heart quickened in excitement. It was nearing the end of the Buffalo Field Campaign's first year. Our job, as volunteers, was to keep the buffalo who strayed from the safety of Yellowstone National Park out of the jurisdiction of the Montana Department of Livestock. If they didn't get to safety before the MDL found them, they would be shot or rounded up and transported to probable death. Years ago I had started the Buffalo Field Campaign, run on grass roots contributions and the help of volunteers from all over the world, because I felt that buffalo are native and sacred to our land. Because the federal and state governments consistently favor cattle over wildlife, I feared for a second extinction of the buffalo and was determined to do something about it. Each winter when buffalo migrate out of the park looking for food, we go out on daily patrols to save them from being harassed and rounded up or killed. Some bison carry a disease called brucellosis, which affects cattle too. When they wander away from the protection of Yellowstone National Park into Montana, the MDL is authorized to round up any strays and check them for the disease and exterminate them if they choose to prevent any possibility that cattle be contaminated. I feel strongly that buffalo are precious, should remain wild and not be harassed for any reason.

Over the years, I've had hundreds of encounters with buffalo. One of the greatest moments of joy I've ever experienced took place in my first year of the campaign. We had spent all grueling winter trying to save buffalo and it was nearly spring. I headed out on the usual 6 a.m. patrol, cross country skiing into an area called Horse Butte only four miles from Yellowstone National Park. I arrived at our monitoring spot and built a large campfire to keep warm in the freezing dawn air. I was up on a high bluff that dropped off steeply to a river bed below. But the heavy morning mist blocked off any view. As the mist began to slowly burn off, in the distance by the river I could see many, many dark shapes. What could they possibly be—elk? When the sun had risen and burned away enough of the mist, I could finally see what the dark shapes were. Buffalo—scores of them! I stood in awe, watching their beauty as a herd in the wild.

Suddenly, with no prompting on my part, they began to move. I realized they were headed up the bluff toward me! I stood very still as one by one they filed past me up the hill. It was then that I realized I had made my blazing fire right on an old trail! As 147 buffaloes (some mothers with calves) walked past within three to five feet of me, I realized that by some inner signal, they knew it was spring and they were migrating back to Yellowstone! It was hard not to whoop with joy and do a victory dance. These were 147 buffalo that the MDL wouldn't get this year. As they quietly and calmly filed past, the buffalo eyed me with no agitation or aggression of any kind. I felt as though I had stepped back in time, into the past of this beautiful land, when millions of wild buffalo covered virtually all of America. I felt that I was a part of their migration, not just with these back to Yellowstone, but symbolically with them all, in a renewal of our land. This moment was an ultimate joy, and an even greater hope. I felt I was fulfilling my purpose of helping to save the sacred buffalo. I was humbly grateful and doubly blessed. —Mike Mease.

Michael S. Mease is a documentary video producer of environmental and human rights issues who spent years of documenting the plight of the last wild herd of buffalo. The final straw for him was when the state of Montana and the Park Service killed 1083 buffalo in 1997, almost one third of the entire Yellowstone herd. He then founded the Buffalo Field Campaign. Michael lives in West Yellowstone, Montana.

—Bison Facts

The proper name of the North American buffalo is bison, the largest land mammal in North America. Before the arrival of the Europeans, there were millions of bison inhabiting the forests and plains. By the late 1880's the bison had been slaughtered and were close to extinction. There are no truly wild bison left in North America. Less than 200,000 remain in the United States, about 10% on government land and 90% on private ranches. In Canada there are about 40,000 bison. Because of its large heart and strong legs, the bison can run at speeds of up to 40 miles per hour for hours on end. Bison may live from 25 to 40 years.

24

Butterfly

The Mirror of Transformation

If Butterfly has chosen to appear to you, it is asking you to encourage that part of yourself that embraces your next adventure: what you will surely become.

Although the dramatic changes of metamorphosis might be challenging, Butterfly spirit approaches the unknown with calm and joyful anticipation. It trusts in the mysteries of life to develop its unique gifts and possibilities. Butterfly spirit believes that even when you creep like a caterpillar, you hold within you the potential of transformation. It patiently accepts the pace of natural evolution and expects inevitably one day to emerge and soar. An encounter with Butterfly spirit is encouraging you to take the many small caterpillar steps to build your chrysalis of self-confidence. Later, in the larger Butterfly world that is still but a dream, you will transcend into glorious flight.

BEWARE of becoming engaged in transient illusory pastimes, without establishing your unique essential work, work that is sincere, grounded, important, and fulfilling.

25

The Butterfly Birth

T DAWN ON A beautiful warm fall day, on the coast of Southern California, I walked out onto our lawn with my husband. I could see the rising sun breaking orange-red through the morning fog. I could see the ocean swelling beyond the cliff, through the swaying eucalyptus trees. All of a sudden, I fell to my knees, breathing deeply and concentrating intently upon the green grass which I clutched in both hands. My husband and older son dropped with me. I was deep in the hard work of birthing my second son.

In the ravine beside our house, a large eucalyptus tree silently stood in the fog. As usual, at this time of year, it was covered from top to bottom with thousands of brilliant orange blossoms. Only these "blossoms" were not flowers, but monarch butterflies! They hung down from each branch of the tree, one upon another, a living link of orange jewels. We called it "the butterfly tree." The monarchs migrated here every year, content to spend most of the winter in or around the same giant tree, a nesting site in the ravine by the sea. Scientists came from all over the country to see the tree and monitor the butterflies.

On this particular morning, however, the entire flock unexpectedly came up from the ravine, fluttering in droves and settling all over our yard, the blankets we had spread, the mid-wives, my family and me. Because I had decided to spend most of my labor outside, I frequently came face to face with these lovely delicate creatures when, at the height of each contraction, I would crumple to the earth. Here I was, in hard labor, covered with the symbol of transformation! Because I had never known butterflies to do this before, I knew how rare and sacred a blessing this was. I believe they had come up from the ravine and the safety of their winter home especially to bless the birth and to share with us the ineffable grace of butterfly magic.

That evening, before a roaring fire in our fireplace, our son was born. Meanwhile, down in the dark ravine, resting quietly one upon another in a giant old eucalyptus tree, were thousands of our gentle orange friends. They had migrated such a long distance to grace my son's birth day with exquisite beauty, and to strengthen his mother when I needed it most, with their extraordinary love. —V.C.

—Butterfly Facts

Millions of monarch butterflies migrate thousands of miles, even over long stretches of water, to winter in warm climates. Native to America, biologists believe that Monarchs may have been doing this for nearly 2 million years! The Monarch is the only one among 50,000 butterfly species that migrates. It is still unknown how the Monarch find their way, without any older generation to lead them, to the same nesting and wintering sites each year. It is believed to be an inherited behavior pattern. During their migration a Monarch is capable of traveling twice as fast as a human can walk. Along the way, it is imperative that they find nutrition to give them enough energy for the long journey. Many people plant special "butterfly gardens" to both attract and help sustain them. Butterflies prefer cornflowers, goldenrod, lupine, marigolds, straw flowers, zinnias, phlox, honeysuckle, frost weeds and butterfly bushes, among other nectar-producing plants. Especially important to the Monarch is milkweed where they lay their eggs. If humans over-develop the resting grounds of the migrating Monarch, or disturb their migratory habitat—even by removing a few crucial trees—the existence of this brilliant flying jewel will be jeopardized.

Coyote

Magical Mischief

If *Coyote* has chosen to appear to you, it is asking you to encourage that part of yourself that holds an unusual perspective and an unpredictable behavior.

oyote spirit is the irreverent, spontaneous, mischievous part of yourself that sees the humorous side of what others take too seriously. Coyote vision combines awareness and lack of ego to become the trickster/magician that uses humor to alter the perception of reality for itself and others. Coyote does not honor strong attachments to roles or positions in life. Coyote provides space between two hardened perceptions of reality, wherein a new possibility may arise. Coyote knows how to see magic and humor everywhere. Can you, by encountering Coyote mischief, laugh at yourself, transforming that which is heavy and serious into that which is light and humorous?

BEWARE of judging the beliefs of others without an underlying appreciation of diversity, and a respect for the sacred.

The Medicine of Three

 HAD ALWAYS WANTED to see a coyote in the wild and up close, because for me the coyote represents a very important part of myself, the wild and free spirit within me that cannot be tamed and the irreverent mischievous part that sees the unusual hidden within life everywhere. I had seen them in a pack at a great distance, seen their numerous tracks in the riverbed sand, and heard them howling in the night many, many times, but I had never had a personal encounter with one. Then one summer, in the space of three weeks, I had three very meaningful encounters. It was these encounters which prompted me to begin writing this book.

The first happened with my younger son, while driving down a meandering mountain road on the way to our favorite swimming spot on the river. We were approaching an empty meadow. There standing in full daylight, looking straight at me, was a sole coyote. He didn't run away as I expected, but continued to stare at us. I drove down the road, but was impelled to turn around and go back. He was still there as we approached, looking calmly over his shoulder at us. I pulled off the road, up next to him. We stayed there watching each other for quite a while. Finally he turned and disappeared into the woods. I felt so honored.

The next encounter occurred the very next week while camping with my two sons. A small coyote slowly crossed in front of the path of our car. We had to slow down to a crawl not to hit him. When we had finally come to a full stop, he ambled up, in very uncharacteristic coyote behavior, along the passenger side of our car and stared directly into the open window at me. If I had just stretched out my arm, I could have touched him. He sat down on the side of the road to stare intently at me before moving into the forest. I was deeply moved.

The final encounter was a week later, when on a trip through the desert, my older son and I came upon a large animal lying dead on the road, with a dead owl nearby. We pulled over to look. Even before my eyes could tell me, I already knew in my heart that it was, of course, a coyote. My son gently pulled him off the road into the flowering sagebrush. Together we felt his soft fur and could tell that he had just

recently been hit. We carried over the owl and kneeled together with them, saying prayers and asking for a blessing for them and from them. We sprinkled them both with pungent desert sage and left them there under the beautiful blue, desert sky. We did not speak for a long while. We knew that we had just been greatly honored and we were humbled before it.

All three encounters were within three weeks, while driving, and all three involved my sons. I have never seen a coyote again. —V.C.

— Coyote Facts

The coyote is a master at hiding, camouflaged by a tawny coat tipped with gray and rust. Yet although coyote is invisible, he misses nothing, endowed with excellent hearing, sight and sense of smell. "Wily coyote" is a well-deserved appellation; many biologists believe that there is no wild animal better at using its brain. The coyote is not only intelligent but resourceful and adaptable as well. For over a hundred years ranchers have been trying to wipe out coyotes for endangering sheep, but a strange phenomena has occurred: wherever coyotes are seriously hunted with intent to exterminate, more of them appear than ever. Many Native Americans believe that if all life on Earth faded away, one creature alone would remain: the coyote.

Deer

The Power of Humility

If Deer has chosen to appear to you, it is asking you to encourage that part of yourself that is not afraid to be soft, gentle and humble.

Deer spirit is the humility to not need to be seen or known, which of itself holds great value when it comes from a place of inner strength. It watches from a hidden place and is quietly aware, not needing to speak what it knows. Deer is the inherent beauty of stillness and simplicity within, a gentle nobility that brings peace to its environment. As humility, deer is the peacekeeper that, through kindness, reinforces the strength and integrity of relationships. Deer does not require appreciation from others to rest elegantly within its own centered place of balance. With Deer you can walk into the deep quiet forest of yourself and seek the sweet, soft, simple part of your nature.

REMEMBER that humility is noble only when it highly values itself, which is not the same as low self-esteem or lack of self worth.

The Deer's Farewell

EARS AGO I HAD the privilege of living for a year in a mountain forest retreat. My little one room cabin was off by itself, high off the ground and nestled amidst seven ancient old growth trees, one of which had fallen over next to my front door. The retreat was very primitive. My cabin had gas heat and a sink with running cold water, but no electricity and no bathroom! There was an outhouse down the trail from my cabin; and in warmer weather, a private outdoor shower without a roof. You could shampoo your hair while looking up through the trees at the sky! Many cold mornings, in nightgown and hiking boots, I would haul heavy buckets of hot water from the shower up the trail to bathe my little boy in the sink in our warm cabin. The year we spent there, while difficult, was also magical. At night while my little boy slept, I would sit on the cabin steps in the pure blackness of the forest, and commune with the ancient trees, singing lullabies to the deer. Each night I would hear one or two of them come, away from the wind and weather, to take shelter underneath the cabin. I would hear and feel their antlers thumping and bumping the floor under my bed. It would comfort me to know they were there with me—that I was not alone in the deep forest.

All year long, conversing with the different deer families who crossed by my cabin, I slowly grew to recognize each individual. The year passed quickly and the year retreat came to an end. Our belongings were packed and good-byes to all our friends were said. Coming up the mountain trail through the quiet forest for the last time, it was through the thick fog that I saw them. It was early dawn and I could barely make them out, standing ghost-like amidst the trees next to my cabin. I set down the heavy pails of hot water I was carrying and stood on the trail in my nightgown, as still as they.

There was magic in this sacred moment. There they were, seven deer, staring at me with their huge soft knowing eyes, not doing anything at all, just waiting. The eldest, with the largest antlers, moved toward me, as if to comfort me as I wept. He stopped, as though not to threaten me, an arm's length away. All of us stood together in this quiet way while I said good-bye and thank you to each of them. For the whole year they had come daily to my cabin in ones and twos; now they were here

all together at dawn on the last morning. They had come to my cabin steps and stood silently waiting amidst the huge trees in the fullness of heart to honor me—and simply say good-bye. Now as the morning mist lifted, the seven quietly moved away into the forest.

How deeply precious, how moving this moment was to me. Feeling the forest watching, I lifted up a smile to my friends, the ancient trees. In my heart where a longing sadness had been, was now the blessing of the trees and the noble grace of the deer's farewell. —V.C.

—Deer Facts

Deer are the most common large wild animal in North America today. A baby fawn is camouflaged by white spots all over its back, which looks to predators like splashes of sunlight on the forest floor. Predators cannot smell fawns, for they are born without any smell for the first week of life. A fawn can stand at birth, and by the end of a week they are able to run. If a doe has two or more fawns, she hides them in different locations so that if a predator finds one, the others are safe. Although generally deer run quickly from predators, doe protecting their fawns have been known to fight off eagles, coyotes, bobcats and mountain lions with their sharp hooves.

Dolphin

The Compassion
To Relieve Suffering

If **Dolphin** has chosen to appear to you, it is asking you to encourage that part of yourself that is committed to caring for the needs of the world.

olphin spirit, swimming in the consciousness of love, views all through a generous heart. Dolphin acutely senses the distress of others and seeks if at all possible to alleviate their pain. It compassionately eases others into balance by helping them to release their grief into an ocean of peace. Dolphin's joyful energy is willing to sacrifice itself to protect and nurture its loved ones. Dolphin spirit is living one's entire life immersed in the "give away" of kindness to others. Dolphin believes that if you possess no other quality but kindness, you have everything.

BEWARE of compassion that remains passive as mere sympathy. True compassion actively reaches out to change the lives of others.

The Dolphin's Gift

HE OCEAN HAS ALWAYS been a big part of my life. My mom used to bring us kids to the beach frequently, believing that the ocean has both a calming and rejuvenating effect. As a young teen, I continued to take trips to the beach, for I was bitten by the surfing bug! Surfing became the passion of my life and that of my buddies. As important as being out in the ocean, surrounded by nature and riding the waves, was the intimate camaraderie of the surfers. We were a family—closer than a family, really—for we shared a common passion and love. I went surfing with my buddies whenever I could; it became a large part of my life. As happens to most young people, as we got older we drifted apart and went our separate ways. I hardly ever surfed any more. I even forgot how exhilarated the ocean made me feel. I forgot how it touched a core primal need to be a part of nature itself.

One beautiful day staring out of my office window at the ocean view, I noticed that the surf was perfect! I realized I was intensely longing for the wild, free and exciting feeling of being out on the waves again. Spontaneously, I left the office and rushed home. I grabbed the old board out of the closet and drove to my favorite surfing spot. Soon I was out all alone in the glorious surf, riding the big waves. Even though I knew it was crazy, I half expected some of my old buddies to show up. How I missed them! They never came, but others showed up—ones I never expected!

After one particular ride, I was paddling back out to the swells when suddenly there was a pod of dolphins rushing toward me! My heart raced. Were they going to be aggressive with me for trespassing on their territory? But they appeared to be unaffected by my presence, for without pausing, they raced by me to catch up with the next big swell! It was a splendid wave and they had timed it perfectly, and rode it gracefully to shore. Before reaching land they flipped on their sides and cut back speedily, right towards me. They surrounded me, flipping all around me excitedly. They began darting side to side in front of me, jumping and spinning through the waves.

They were magnificent surfers and I marveled at their graceful turns and perfect cutbacks. Their moves were precise, powerful and in perfect rhythm with each wave. They vocalized to one another after each ride as they headed back out through the white water. It was as if they were sharing with each other the experience—their stories and successes—exactly as my buddies and I had done together so many years ago. How I envied them. How lonely I felt for my old friends. But gradually, as I continued to surf among them, I felt invited into their group. They made me feel that I was a part of their community, as much as any human could be. I was very aware

that I was experiencing something extraordinary and deeply spiritual. My soul was filled with inspiration and exhilaration. The dolphin's joy was contagious—I had never felt so alive!

When the dolphins finally disappeared, I sat for a long time on my board and laughed out loud. By sharing their joyful nature with me and including me in our favorite pastime, I realized that I no longer felt lonely. I too, was part of the glorious community on planet Earth. I too, a fellow creature of the ocean along with the dolphins, was part of the joyous celebration dance of the sea. —Brian Weisman.

Brian Weisman is an animal training supervisor and civilian consultant on the health, welfare, and training of Atlantic bottlenose dolphins. He has been training dolphins for the U.S. Navy for 15 years.

—Dolphin Facts

Dolphins are masters of the acoustical world, both in hearing and emitting sounds. Dolphins can make many sounds, among them whistling, buzzing, clicking, popping, mewing, and squealing, as well as many others sounds that are beyond the audible frequencies for humans. Dolphins in water, similar to bats in the air, are well known for their ability to echolocate which allows them to detect and follow objects under water. They emit loud clicking noises and can accurately interpret the returning echoes. They can even determine by echolocation whether an object is solid or hollow. Their high pitched whistle, among other sounds, seems to be an important carrier of social information. Each dolphin appears to have a "signature" whistle that transmits its identity.

Eagle

Nobility

If Eagle has chosen to appear to you, it is asking you to encourage that part of yourself that enhances character through integrity and self-mastery.

agle spirit leads others onto their own path of truth by exemplifying values that bring honor: integrity, equality, independence, loyalty, and endurance. While rooted in tradition, Eagle uses its strong wings to soar into the skies of invention, achieving a more expansive vision for the larger community. With determined will, Eagle strives to achieve the highest caliber of self-mastery. Dignified Eagle understands that nobility embodied in even one individual, although perhaps unseen, increases the quality of life for all on Earth. If you encounter Eagle, you are being urged to stand up to all opposition and strongly uphold your highest values of integrity.

BEWARE of false nobility, which rooted in the ego parades as the dignity of pride; it is no substitute for developing a quiet inner dignity.

The Eagle's Gift

ONE WINTER DAY, I was recovering from a long illness, and needing inspiration, I drove by a favorite place, a lake where years earlier I had spotted an osprey in a dead pine tree. This was a precious spot to me because I had made a promise that day, to the osprey and myself, to save its home. That sighting two years earlier had led me to help establish the first preserve dedicated to biodiversity in North America, the Finger Lakes Land Trust Biodiversity Preserve in upstate New York. This valuable land—a mixture of forest, fields and marshes—is a highly varied landscape with incredible plant, animal, and habitat diversity.

As an adopted member of the Seneca-Iroquois Hawk clan, I feel it is my duty and privilege to help preserve as many ancient forests as I can. So I urged the Land Trust to save this unique wild place before it was lost to development forever. Thankfully, the Land Trust agreed and we were able to raise the funds necessary to purchase it, turning it into a nature preserve for posterity.

On this day, however, my thoughts were not on ospreys, but on eagles. I thought that this would be a perfect place for eagles to come. It was then that I noticed a large white flash in the very same tree across the lake. Because it was March, I thought maybe it was just a patch of snow, or a broken-off branch, but no, it was the head of a bald eagle! Ill or not, I was soon headed across a field around the lake, in the direction of the eagle. I hoped for a closer contact, but the eagle, spotting me, took off and flew right over me. Its beauty and power took my breath away and tears of joy came down my face.

I continued toward the tree, hoping for a gift left behind, such as a feather. But when I arrived at the base of the tree, I saw no feather or anything else. I was turning to leave, when something caught my eye. There, directly under the tree, was the empty shell of a large snapping turtle. I picked it up and held it in my hands, turning it over and over in amazement and awe. What a gift— perfect beyond belief! In the Iroquois tradition the Earth is "Turtle Island" and our most honored symbol is the image of a great turtle with a pine tree on its back, its roots covering the turtle, and on the top of the tree is perched an eagle. This is exactly what I had beheld that day.

I brought the turtle shell home to my hawk clan grandmother, a true medicine woman, and told her my story. She looked up at me through aged eyes of wisdom and in a low voice said "this is real medicine from the eagle—meant just for you—for saving its home." I felt blessed to be seen as worthy to receive such medicine. I like to think that perhaps it is also the land's gift back to me for helping to preserve it for all generations to come. The Turtle Island nation is rooted in the Earth, held sacred for all time and yet soars free like an eagle in my heart. —Michael DeMunn / Da Hah' da' nyah: in Seneca Iroquois meaning, "he protects the forest."

Michael DeMunn is a forester and founder of the Finger Lakes Land Trust, a 1,000 member conservation organization in central New York. He has helped save thousands of acres of important wild lands including rare old-growth forests that were about to be logged. He has worked with many organizations including the Forest Service, The Nature Conservancy, and the American Indian Network. He is also an environmental educator who gives programs for schools, conservation groups, and others. He is author of the award-winning book Places of Power *(Dawn Publications) and* The Earth is Good.

— Eagle Facts

An eagle is a raptor, a word derived from the Latin raptare, meaning "to seize or grasp," because raptors catch prey with their feet. Eagles have excellent eyesight. It is believed that an eagle is able to see a rabbit from nearly two miles away. Their eyes are larger than those of a human. It has three protective lids, including a "nictitating membrane" that closes sideways across the eye. The eagle can actually see perfectly well through this eyelid, even though the eyes appear to be closed. Due to pesticides, over-hunting and habitat destruction, there were fewer than 1,000 nesting individuals in the lower 48 states by the 1960's and the eagle was declared an endangered species. In one of the great success stories of our time, there are now 8,000 nesting eagles in the lower 48 states, and tens of thousands of eagles in Alaska and Canada.

Frog

Adaptability

If FROG has chosen to appear to you, it is asking you to encourage that part of yourself that is not only open to change but understands its benefits.

Frog spirit reflects the fundamental principle that all life evolves and that nothing ever remains constant. Frog knows that what seems strange today, may very well be a comfortable reality tomorrow. Frog spirit calls out to shift your perception of your experience and not fear that which is different. It patiently embraces a spacious awareness of unmanifested potential. Frog encourages you to let go of the past, of stages and environments that you have outgrown. If you encounter Frog spirit, it is urging you to release that which no longer serves you, blessing it with peace, and to approach with calm acceptance that which you will now become.

BEWARE of letting go of the precious parts of yourself merely because another thinks you should.

FROG MAN

HEN I WAS VERY young, they used to call me "turtle boy," because my favorite pastime was catching turtles. I could watch turtles and frogs for hours, day after day. Often there would be eight to nine turtles on one log together. On hands and knees I would stalk them, so quietly, so carefully, taking my time however long it took. When I felt I was finally "in tune" with them, I would make the snatch! Triumphantly, with one in each hand, I would take them home and make whole environments out on the lawn for them, including little "ponds." But invariably, when I woke up the next morning, I would find that they had escaped, every last one of them! So I would have to start the whole process all over again. It was the same with frogs. Throughout my entire youth, I was just crazily in love with turtles and frogs. Years went by and I just could never get enough of them.

When I became a grown man, with children of my own, my life was definitely on a different pattern. No matter how slowly or stealthily I would creep up on the pond, the frogs would always hear me. Before I could even get sight of them, I would hear them plopping everywhere into the water. I kept wondering, "What's the deal? Have the frogs and turtles changed? Have the new generations become more savvy? Or is it just that I have changed? Have I become so out of touch with the natural world?" And then one summer day I had a life opening experience.

I had taken out an old inflated inner tube I found lying in the shed and floated out on it, alone, into the center of a neighboring pond, deep in the woods. Gradually I grew more and more peaceful. The fast pace of the world faded and the dreamlike pace of the pond pulled me into its magic, lulling me into a deep calm. I idly paddled around, watching the treetops catch the clouds in their arms, the dragonflies hatch and the red-wing blackbirds alight in the rustling cattails. I became so in tune with the pond that I became the pond.

It was then that I noticed many, many pairs of eyes watching me. All over the pond. Big bulging frog eyes. And it seemed they were all looking right at me. Turtle boy's heart raced, but calmly I drifted over closer to one large frog and stopped a few feet away. I didn't want to frighten him. We stared at each other intently. The frog didn't move, so I chanced moving a little closer. I noticed how beautiful he was—what amazing colors! The frog continued to watch me, unmoving, still as stone. Finally, holding my breath, I reached out with one finger. I reached and reached and then—I touched his nose! I was astounded! And yet, he still didn't move. Why? He continued to stare at me peacefully. I thought, "I'm no longer 'turtle boy stalker,' I am 'frog man'"! I was actually having a respectful relationship with this little frog being! When the frog finally disappeared beneath the water, I tried it again with another frog. And it worked again—over and over!

After that, I made time every day to go to the pond to commune with the frogs. I would sit for long periods of time, not trying to grasp or clutch them in my hand, as I had done so long ago, but instead quietly examining every unique facet of them. I would simply appreciate their unique beauty from a distance, not trying to possess them as captives. I guess "turtle boy" had finally grown up. I liked the man he had become: a man who, by merely touching the nose of a frog, had been given by the frog in return the valuable gift of touching his heart. —Mark McNair.

Mark McNair lives with his family in an 1830s farmhouse by a broad creek on the Chesapeake Bay. When he is not pursuing his artistic career, you will find him drifting in his boat, fishing and exploring the edges of the sea.

—Frog Facts

A frog is an amphibian who goes through the miraculous process of metamorphosis. "Amphibian" comes from two ancient Greek words, amphi (both) and bios (life), because a typical amphibian spends its larval stage (eggs and tadpole) in water and its adult (frog) stage mostly or totally on land. "Metamorphosis" is also derived from two ancient Greek words meaning "many changes." Most frogs lay their eggs in a clear jelly in shallow water near the surface, where it is warm. There are always exceptions, of course! For example, the tiny green male Darwin's frog holds its eggs and young in its mouth—vocal pouch—until they are old enough to look out for themselves, when the father releases them. One theory as to why amphibian populations are in serious decline, besides loss and alteration of local habitat, is the effect of ultraviolet radiation on the developing eggs. These are the same UV rays that are increasingly causing skin cancers in humans. Also of serious concern is the large numbers of deformed frogs being born all over North America. Many species of frogs are known to be sensitive environmental indicators.

Hawk

Intuition, Clarity of Insight

If Hawk has chosen to appear to you, it is asking you to encourage that part of yourself that is intuitively aware.

Hawk spirit uses its powerful intuition to sense with clarity all around, all within, and all that lies in the future. Intuition is the voice of the soul, which always speaks radical truth. Intuitive Hawk sight soars high, seeing far into the future; and dives deep, delving far into the soul. Hawk power observes everything with keen awareness, simultaneously focusing with fierce clarity your own inner sight. Is there a time when you listened to your intuition and it guided you correctly—or when you didn't, and wished you had? Hawk spirit flies over you as a forceful reminder to listen and trust your inner messages.

REMEMBER that clarity of sight sees what is before the eyes, but clarity of insight—true vision—comes from behind the eyes.

The Fallen Nest

NCE WHEN I WAS living on a small island off the Gulf Cost, two ospreys (fish hawks) decided to build a nest next to my house, which was only steps away from the water. Ospreys always build huge nests of sticks in the highest location available, way up in the air. This couple decided to build their nest in the television antenna of my neighbors, not uncommon to see on an island landscape. From my deck, twelve feet above the ground, I had a perfect view of their constant hard labor. Not only did they have to find the right size sticks and bring them back to the nest site, but once there, they had to "weave" them securely into the nest so that they could hold the weight of two adults and perhaps two chicks.

Daily I would cheer them on. Barely able to fly with the weight of a large stick, the ospreys would land and place it carefully on the growing nest, sometimes only to have it fall 35 feet to the ground when it became unbalanced, even bringing several other sticks with it! As the ospreys watched helplessly as all their hard work disintegrated in front of them, they would look over intently at me, as if they expected me to somehow retrieve the sticks. (If I had been able to, I probably would have!) I had the distinct feeling that these were new parents: first time builders who were learning through practice what would work and what wouldn't. Finally, after hundreds of trips, they appeared content with their structure, now a huge, unwieldy bowl of branches, about five feet across. I would see them arriving all through the day with a fish, often still flapping in their talons, to perch on the edge of the nest and eat.

One day some inner sense told me the eggs had been laid. Sure enough, the parents were taking turns sitting and going out to collect fish. When the brood hatched, the parents were constantly busy feeding their chicks. I called out my congratulations, and closely monitored the constant activity. I was so proud of them.

But one day a huge tropical storm hit, with trees thrashing as if in a hurricane. I was so worried about the nest and the nestlings, I couldn't take my eyes away from the window, anxiously watching every violent gust. And then my worst fear happened. In loud gale that sounded like a train coming through the neighborhood, the huge nest toppled and the entire structure landed in the yard, smashed. Crying out, I ran outside to where the nest lay. It was immense! I moved the branches

aside, and lying on the ground with their small talons curled up, were two fuzzy chicks, dead. Filled with despair, I wept. What could I do? The two parent ospreys swooped down again and again, intently peering and peering. After the storm had passed, I stood up on our deck in the wind, calling and reaching out to them. For an hour the parents repeatedly circled over my head, staring down at the fallen nest, crying and crying, with a sound I had never heard them make before. I mourned with them, returning to them the same keening sound. When my son came home from school, he lovingly wrapped the little chicks and buried them in the woods with prayers. The parent ospreys never returned to build a nest in the television antenna again. —V.C.

—Hawk Facts

If you find a bird of prey (raptor) chick that is unharmed, place it up high out of danger near where you found it. After you leave, its cries may draw the parents who may have been nearby watching. If the raptor is hurt, covering its head with a cloth will calm it. Pick up the bird with gloved hands, holding its wings and legs together where the legs meet the body. Put it into a covered cardboard box and take it to the nearest wildlife rescue center or raptor rehabilitation center, humane society, state wildlife office or a willing veterinarian.

Mountain Lion

The Spirit of Independence

If Mountain Lion has chosen to appear to you, it is asking you to encourage that part of yourself that self-sufficiently explores the mysteries of solitude.

Cougar spirit has loosened any attachment to permanence, engaging in a whole-hearted relationship with independence. Even when its environment pushes in on all sides, Mountain Lion is masterful in maintaining genuine wildness. Never following the crowd, Mountain Lion is fulfilled in being alone. It seeks out solitude so that it may hear messages from the transforming silence. Its independent ideas can never be tamed. Mountain Lion is asking you to examine the quality of your self-esteem, which is essential to true independence. If you have had the rare opportunity of a physical sighting, be on the lookout for a big change. Regardless of how your encounter with Mountain Lion takes place, you are being encouraged to follow your instincts fearlessly and trust in your own empowered ideas.

BEWARE of self-involved egotistical energy that forgets to help empower others.

A Test of Heart

NCE WHEN I WAS out on a solo backpacking trip in a wilderness area, I stumbled into the camp site of an older man who was resting alone beside a campfire. Because neither of us had seen any people for several days, we were glad to have a chance to talk, and he invited me to join his campfire. After we had shared our personal stories for a while, he told me the most amazing story I had ever heard, not the expected campfire yarn, but an emotional recital of heartfelt experience.

A few years earlier he had been in the midst of a "middle age crisis" and was deeply pondering what to do in the next phase of his life. He had decided that the best way to proceed was to learn how to open himself up to the deepest source of his own love. So he took a long solo trip into the mountains to do this "heart-work" and then see what would come from having increased his ability to love. For many days he roamed the pristine wilderness, working on opening up his heart, and expanding his own concept of how to truly love unconditionally. He concentrated entirely on this exercise and each day he could feel his heart opening more fully. He achieved a place of joy within that he had never known existed. His body began to hum with joy, to vibrate with love.

One day, after a few weeks in the woods, as he approached an area of wilderness where he had never been before, a mountain lion appeared from out of the shadows of the forest, and stood face to face with him on the path. At that moment, because of the man's intensive heart work, he was able to feel complete love rather than terror. Standing his ground, the man felt his heart brimming over with admiration for this beautiful creation of God. Somehow he knew that this was his test—the one he had come searching for.

Suddenly the lion ran toward him and, leaping several feet through the air, pounced on him, knocking him to the ground! Placing her heavy weight on the man's chest, the great cat proceeded to tenderly lick the man's face! With mischief in her eyes, she began to bat gently at the man with her paws, encouraging him to play! He was astonished and began to laugh and actually began playing with the mountain lion. Man and cougar then continued hiking together as companions for over a week, sharing many adventures. Finally he had to return to civilization and his

life, which would never be the same—how could it? Even more amazing, was that when he returned a year later to this same wilderness site, the mountain lion again appeared and they renewed their close, loving relationship, again living side by side for more than a week.

It's been years since I've heard that story, but I still love to think about it. —Michael Eller

Michael Eller is a professional wilderness guide. See his story, "Dancing with Bears," on page 14.

—Mountain Lion Facts

The mountain lion is at once everywhere and nowhere. Once upon a time it had the widest distribution of any single mammal species in the Western Hemisphere. It lived in nearly every state, adapting to life in mountains, deserts, coastal forests, sub-alpine forests, swamps, woodlands, and prairies. Mountain lions, also known as panthers, pumas, American lion, catamounts and cougars, are considered the "ghosts of North America." They are now found only in isolated pockets. They cannot be observed from a distance or from a blind, nor readily approached. A sighting is extremely rare.

Mustang

Freeing Your Own Wildness

If Mustang has chosen to appear to you, it is asking you to encourage that part of yourself that holds on to the bond of wildness.

ustang has both the conviction and the stamina to maintain its independence, no matter how hard others seek to tame or corral it. Mustang spirit, the passion fire of soul, moves with inherent beauty, one with the wind. It also has the native strength to stand its ground for what it must protect: its right and privilege to be free. The wild horse is your connection with the river of untamed passion that runs within you, and your vigorous choice to maintain it. If you encounter Mustang, it is a challenge to keep the wildness within alive, and a warning not to let others change you into who you are not.

REMEMBER that true freedom is found not in running fearfully away from something, but in the power of passionately moving toward something.

The Dun Stallion

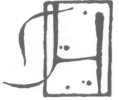ORSES POSSESS AN ALMOST preternatural ability to fascinate even young children. I was thoroughly enchanted by them when I was four. I was much older when my ingenuous love for them was replaced with a commitment to their well being and protection. And I owe this commitment to a single wild horse.

For more than ten years I had been camping in the White Mountain Range of Wyoming. On my first visit in July 1989, I was quite taken with a band of wild horses under the direction of a magnificent dun stallion. He had "zebra" markings around his fetlocks and a primitive dorsal stripe. His mane and tail were exceptionally long and his forelock came half way down the front of his face, gracing a perfectly sculpted Roman nose—a testament to his regal Spanish heritage. When he asserted his authority, he delivered a collected trot that rivaled that of a well-schooled dressage horse.

After four summers of admiring this band through binoculars, I decided it was time to have a closer look. I found them in their usual grazing territory. True to their nature, they were very much aware of my intrusion long before I spotted them. I parked my truck about a mile from their range, and proceeded on foot. Each time one of the horses raised a head, I froze to avoid scaring them off. Finally the stallion had had enough of me. He shot his head up, pranced around, flashed his tail wildly and then charged! I stood my ground and waved my arms violently to divert him. Luckily, this tactic worked—he stopped dead in his tracks. After a few minutes, he slowly began to circle me, while continuing to maintain his distance. When he was satisfied that I was not a threat, he matter-of-factly returned to his mares and resumed grazing.

That night I camped on a small precipice. At dawn I was awakened by a loud blowing noise outside my tent. The stallion! Without thinking, I ripped open the tent zipper and startled him. He galloped to the far side of my truck, turned and stood looking at me over the hood. In my haste to get out of the tent, I was dressed only in my underwear and hiking boots! He tossed his head and knickered softly, half beckoning at me to come forward, half warning me not to try anything foolish.

I walked up to my truck, slowly reached my arm over the hood and offered him my hand. In turn, he stretched his neck and extended his nose to take in my scent. Only a hair's breadth of space hung between my fingertips and his nose. The temptation to touch him was overwhelming, but I remained content to revel in our intimacy without contact. Ours was a silent communion that transcended the spoken word. After several minutes he turned calmly and trotted down the small embankment to his mares. As he began herding them away, he turned to me and tossed his head. I raised my hand and whispered, "Good bye to you too."

The following summer I searched in vain for the stallion and his band. I never saw them again. Perhaps he surrendered his band to a tougher, younger stallion. This would be nature's law. But it was 1994 and the Bureau of Land Management was "waging war" against Wyoming's wild horses. I fear he was rounded up, branded and gelded, and forced to serve some human whim in captivity. I am glad I was not the human who first touched him. I think of the dun stallion often and in my dreams I run with him across the White Mountain Range, just one of the band, wild and free. —Robin Duxbury.

Robin Duxbury is co-founder of Project Equus, www. projectequus.org, a national horse protection organization with headquarters in Boulder, Colorado. Project Equus works to prevent horse abuse in competitive equestrian sports. Duxbury is a private investigator who works undercover to identify abusive horse trainers for law enforcement agencies. As a court-certified expert witness on horse training, she assists District Attorneys to prosecute abusive trainers.

— Mustang Facts

Horses have been on Earth since the time of the dinosaurs, evolving and living in the wild over most of North America, migrating to Asia, Africa and Europe over the Bering land bridge when the species was the size of a cat. Eight to ten thousand years ago they died out in North America. The Spanish explorers brought them back to the Americas in the 1500s. Some of those domesticated horses escaped and remain wild, called "mustangs" by the Spanish (which means "strayed" or "wild"). It is estimated that mustang herds in America once numbered about eight million, but were reduced to a mere 20,000. They were slaughtered for use as pet food, or killed by ranchers who did not want them to compete with cattle for grazing land. Currently, there are approximately 40,000 wild horses living in ten western U.S. states, mostly in Nevada, plus some on islands off Maryland and Nova Scotia. Over very long distances mustangs can outrun anything, even thoroughbred horses with their longer legs that have been bred for racing.

Otter

An Inner Source of Joy

If *Otter* has chosen to appear to you, it is asking you to encourage that part of yourself that lives with a joyful heart.

he playful Otter spirit is spontaneously lively and perpetually cheerful. Otter understands that joy is the rejuvenating force of life, and enthusiastically seeks the delight hidden within every experience. It dives again and again into the unknown. As an active optimist, it perceives the vital gift of each precious moment and offers that gift creatively to others. Rich in devotion to its loved ones, it offers whole-hearted and concentrated affection. If you encounter Otter spirit, it is asking you to arouse your healing gift of laughter and playfulness, to encourage or inspire another.

BEWARE of mindlessly playing your life away without making a valuable contribution.

A Mama's World

HEN I WAS TWO months pregnant with my second son, my husband and I hiked out into a rocky ocean cove on the Big Sur coast of Northern California. Filling the cove were thick mats of floating kelp. Forests of brown fibrous seaweed shifted sensuously with each wave. Carefully we climbed down rocky bluffs, narrow trails and slippery ledges to get closer to the ocean's edge. We sat on a rocky precipice and looked at the quiet cove.

As we sat quietly, appreciating the beauty of the rugged coastline with its thick forest of pine trees marching down to the water's edge, we noticed continuous movement amidst the kelp bed. Then as our eyes adjusted, we gasped to see little brown furry heads with cute little beady eyes popping up and down throughout the entire cove. There, perfectly camouflaged by the kelp, making only subtle movements, were dozens of otters lying on their backs throughout the cove. They appeared to be totally unconcerned by our presence so near. But, what were they doing, we wondered? Snoozing in the sun? Basking in the warmth? And what was that on their bellies? Lunch? I knew they ate a strict diet of conch, but this didn't look like conch, and it didn't look as if they were eating, but washing. Washing what? We wished we had brought our binoculars.

Finally, we realized that we were in an otter nursery! Each otter was a mama grooming a tiny baby otter, who was safely riding the swells, snuggled on her belly. Occasionally, the mama otter would place the baby on a large kelp leaf, and—with my heart pounding at least—she would disappear for what seemed forever, only to pop up with lunch and a little squeak a minute later. Rolling onto her back, she placed the baby on her furry tummy and proceeded to eat her meal on top of its

head! This was repeated over and over, throughout the whole community. We watched for hours, never tiring of witnessing one of nature's most precious miracles. I was thrilled and held my own miracle tenderly, stroking my belly and communicating to my baby what I was seeing. What a wonderful omen, to be holding my own baby, surrounded by the company of loving otter mamas. — V.C.

— Otter Facts

A mother sea otter's devotion to her pup is strongly emotional and physical, with constant affection. When it is time to nap, a mother sea otter will often hold paws with her youngster, as it floats beside her, in order to stay together. The mothering instinct in a female sea otter is so strong that if while diving below for food, she loses her cub to a predator such as an eagle, she will search for her baby for days, even adopting a motherless cub as her own. The sea otter lives its entire life in the ocean, eating, sleeping, birthing and rearing its young.

Owl

Introspection

If *Owl* has chosen to appear to you, it is asking you to encourage that part of yourself that, because of inner awareness, is centered within.

wl spirit understands everything with wisdom because it has made a priority of taking the time to introspect and to know itself first. Owl sits quietly as mirror to itself, watching from a secure place of introspection. Owl spirit sees in all directions, even in darkness. It understands itself as one with all life. It views many perspectives, even while it is intensely focused inward. By remaining in integrity, it has taken control of its own destiny. Owl, as the center of its universe, owns the forest. Owl is a wake-up call to open your eyes and look within. Encountering Owl can also signify that one facet of your life is coming to a close, and that with inner awareness you will safely take a step forward into your next experience.

BEWARE of becoming so inwardly focused on the gratification of your own desires that you cease to see or care for the realities and needs of others.

Spirit Guides

LL OF MY CHILDHOOD, I grew up exploring the gentle woods throughout New England. When I was 19, my parents moved west, and we decided that I would drive one of the family cars with a couple of my girlfriends across country. It would give me a chance to experience the American West up close for the first time. I could never have guessed the welcome from Spirit Animals of the Wild West that awaited me.

We took a northern route, camping across Canada and the upper mid-western states. When we reached Wyoming, we decided to go for a backpacking trip in the Grand Tetons. We talked to rangers for advice, gathered supplies, packed and started up a long hard trail into the wilderness. One morning, after two splendid days, I headed out on the trail ahead of the others to have some quiet time alone. I knew they would eventually catch up, as there was only one trail. After an hour, I sat down next to the trail in a meadow to catch my breath and take in the immense beauty of the glorious mountain view before me.

Suddenly, there was a great crashing sound behind me. I jumped up and came face to face with a huge wapiti, a male elk, with a full rack of antlers! To this Connecticut Yankee (who had seen plenty of New England deer) he looked like a giant moose! He had burst out of the woods into the meadow and startled us both. We looked at each other for a long moment and then he charged back into the forest. With my heart pounding, I ran to follow him. Then I saw a flash of pure white light farther in the dark forest. What could that be?

Curious, I went deeper in, climbing over boulders and fallen trees with my heavy backpack. I was so busy looking down that I was startled by a sound, or rather more of a feeling, of something watching me from above. I looked up and there, sitting on a dead branch and intently staring down at me, was the largest owl I had ever seen. It was a snowy owl—pure white—like a ghostly spirit. My breath sucked in and my heart felt as if it had stopped beating. Time stopped as we looked at one another. Then the owl, as if in slow motion, took off right in front of me, gliding through the thick dark forest, wings outstretched with maybe a 6 foot wing span. He passed me at shoulder level, making absolutely no sound at all. I stood there for a long moment, stunned, and then made my way back out to the trail to find my friends and tell them what I had seen.

I met them right where I had been sitting earlier, looking at the view, but before I could tell them my story, I saw that they were looking intently down at something.

There on the trail, right where I had been sitting, was a huge track. It was so fresh that puddle water was still trickling into it, filling it up! But it was not elk print—not with those huge claw marks! We didn't have to be outdoorswomen to recognize bear tracks—in an area where there are many grizzlies! You have never seen four girls run so fast.

I've always liked to think that the bull elk and the snowy owl were spirit guides sent to protect and guide me. By luring me with mysterious and captivating beauty away from my seat right in the path of an oncoming bear, they not only protected me but also helped place me on a life-long path—the quest for wildness. Even to this day when I find myself amidst a crowd on a busy city street, I sometimes close my eyes and suddenly, I am gliding through a dark forest glen, on the back of a large snow white owl. Effortlessly we wing through the trees and then disappear, ghostlike, together. No tracks have been left on the forest floor and no sound has been heard in the still mountain air. —V.C.

Rabbit

Wonder Through Innocence

If Rabbit has chosen to appear to you, it is asking you to encourage that part of yourself that is full of wonder at the natural beauty of life.

Rabbit spirit is kind and open-hearted, appreciating the quiet strength of gentleness. Gentleness is sometimes mistakenly perceived as weakness, but in fact it takes greater courage to remain soft and innocent than to be strong and wise. Rabbit, seeing the world through eyes of wonder, is capable of liberating the kindness hidden within others. Sometimes when Rabbit appears to you, it is a mourning for the sweet innocent part of yourself that you have temporarily lost. Encountering Rabbit, it is time to look into your heart. Is your innocence buried deep under layers of hurt, anger and mistrust? Rabbit encourages you to take courage and let your innocent wonder be radiantly revealed once again.

BEWARE of lapsing into a fear that paralyzes you into non-action.

Raccoon

The Courage to Explore the Unknown

If Raccoon has chosen to appear to you, it is asking you to encourage that part of yourself that uses curiosity as a tool to stimulate movement into new areas of growth

accoon is the spirit of masterful inventiveness that energetically seeks out novel experiences and determinedly examines them for fresh possibilities. Self-sufficient Raccoon spirit never waits passively for the unknown to come to it. Rather, it actively reaches out to engage in a dynamic relationship with what its explorations have revealed. Raccoon uses its extreme sensitivity to feel when and where to go, and when to stop and explore a different path. After encountering Raccoon, you now pursue your excellent creativity with vital intention, challenging the formless into form.

BEWARE of superficial curiosity in every passing interest, which robs you of the opportunity to develop deeper knowledge of any.

Live Free, Return to the Wild

HEN I WAS A young boy, a friend of mine gave me a baby raccoon. As she grew, the raccoon and I did everything together, including walks far into the woods and across the fields to the small town in upstate New York near where I lived. I carried her up on my shoulder as I went around in the local grocery story. Everyone, even the store owners, got a big kick out of it whenever I came in with her. As you can imagine, we grew very close, like family. When summer came, I took her to the creek and she just loved it, looking for crawfish and minnows. She would feel around in the mud and gravel for anything that would interest a curious raccoon. When I said, "Come on, let's go," she would come running up and climb up my pants leg until I put her on my shoulder.

But as summer wore on, I began to see it wasn't right for her to be a pet. She was originally a wild animal and should return to the wild. The forest needed her more than I did and I had no right to keep her from living free like all wild creatures are meant to be. Even though this decision tore at my heart, I knew it was the right thing to do. I was determined to help her go wild again. She, however, had other ideas.

She was a year old now and in prime health, and I decided the creek was the perfect place for the raccoon to reclaim a wild life. Taking her down to the creek was easy. But when I attempted to leave without her, it presented a problem. While she was busy fishing, I sneaked a little way up the path toward home. When she noticed I wasn't in sight, she ran after me up the path as fast as she could, and climbed right up my body, as if it was a tree! She sat on my head, holding on as tightly as she could, and chattered loudly at me, scolding me all the way home. Thereafter, whenever we would go to the creek, she would watch me closely. Every time I would try to leave her, she wouldn't stand for it. Gradually, however, she became more and more confident and would stay for a while at the creek after I left. Yet, invariably, much to my discouragement, she showed up at night to sleep curled up in our warm house.

Finally, just when I was about to give up on the whole idea, she didn't return as usual one night. At dawn the next day, I hurried anxiously down to the creek, thinking fearful thoughts. "What if she's been attacked by another animal or even killed? Maybe I should never have tried this experiment, maybe I hadn't prepared her enough, maybe this decision was the wrong one." Then I arrived at the creek and there she was—healthy and happy to see me. She rushed up to me eagerly, chattering a greeting, but I noticed that she didn't touch me. I could see that she wasn't hungry or afraid. I was so relieved. My heart perked up. Maybe there was hope after all. That morning she came home with me and I took her back to the creek later in the day to

spend the night on her own. This pattern repeated for several weeks, when one morning, arriving at the creek, she wasn't there. She had gone off on her own at last. Was she still alive? I hoped and prayed that she made it. In my heart though, a little doubt always nagged at me.

Then one day, many months later, I visited the creek. As usual, I kept an eye out for her. I heard a noise high up in a nearby tree; there, camouflaged in some high branches, were two large raccoons staring intently at me with their big bright eyes—and I was almost certain that one of them was her. The one who looked like her started chattering at me, and then I was sure. Soon the two raccoons climbed down and wandered off into the forest. Before she disappeared, she turned around to look at me as if to say good-bye one last time. My heart swelled. I had done the right thing and it had worked out. Maybe one day next year I would see her with a family of her own. The raccoon was free now, living on her own in the wild. And in that moment I too became free. —Michael DeMunn.

Michael DeMunn is a forester and founder of the Finger Lakes Land Trust. Please also see his story, "The Eagle's Gift," on page 42. (see page 42)

— RACCOON FACTS

Raccoons are said to have the same credo as Americans: "What can be done, ought to be done." They are extremely clever at solving problems, as anyone who has ever assembled a "raccoon-proof" garbage bin can attest. The Algonquin tribe called raccoons arakunen—"he who scratches with his hands." The inquisitive raccoon enjoys handling everything it encounters. They have extraordinary memories and in laboratory tests score higher than rats. The raccoon is capable of remembering what it has learned years earlier. They are extremely successful adapters, and even though there were approximately five million raccoons at the time of the European arrival on the North American continent, their present day number, spread over all environments including cities, now greatly exceeds that. Raccoons are one of the few wild species in North America that have thrived despite modern development.

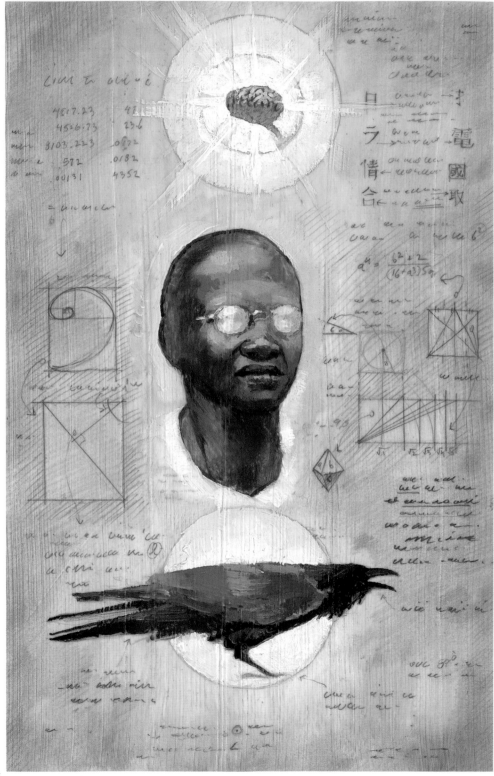

Raven

The Gift of Intelligence

If Raven has chosen to appear to you, it is asking you to encourage that part of yourself that has the ability to understand anything that you set your mind to.

aven is the "can do" spirit that never accepts limitations. It never gives up on what it doesn't yet know, believing that with persistence it will be able to learn the solution to every question. It accepts challenges with relish, enjoying the voyage of discovery as much as the final achievement. When Raven has a setback, it merely intensifies its focus and tries again. Raven comes to tell you that you can trust your own intelligence and have faith in your own excellent ideas. If, when encountering Raven, there is a facet of your life that you have difficulty with, try bringing to it Raven's determined decision of intelligence.

BEWARE of feeling superior to or more special than others, because of your own gifts.

Beyond The Horizon

WHILE WRITING THIS BOOK, I received the stunning news that my youthful, vibrant mother had only weeks to live. In shock, I stumbled helplessly out into a nearby forest meadow. Kneeling to the earth, I tried to grasp on to any clear thought; but my body heaved with sobs. I began to drown in a realm of grief. Finally, exhausted, I became so absorbed in a katydid that landed like a green jewel on my knee, that I didn't see the arrival of three very large ravens near me. Or had they always been there?

They stood, shifting from foot to foot, intensely watching me with dark thoughtful eyes. Eventually, after a visual stand-off, they began to pick at things in the grass. With a gasp I realized that they represented my mother, my father, and me. Since my birth, we three had always been a team, continuously exploring the metaphysical world on a keen quest for wisdom. Sometimes, when one of us would advance a little ahead of the others, the other two would hustle to keep up; and thus we always managed to stay together, hand-in-hand. And now here was my mother, preparing to move off on a journey of her own, leaving my Dad and me here alone. How could this be?

I couldn't take my eyes off the ravens. Then unexpectedly one of them, for no apparent reason, flew into the air and rapidly disappeared over the treetops. The other two watched her leave and then, jumping up together onto a mossy stone wall, calmly began to explore the new area together. No loss—only a new arrangement temporarily. I was stunned at the message the ravens had come to give me.

Then I remembered an analogy for death that my mother had taught me as a little girl when standing on the ocean shore. She said that when a seagull flew beyond the horizon and disappeared from sight, it was not gone but merely experiencing a new reality, apart from our view. For the first time that day, I felt calm come over me and I knew that somehow, some way, my Dad and I would eventually be OK. And so would our beautiful partner who, though soon to be moving ahead of us, would surely wait patiently for us to one day catch up.

The two ravens had moved away from me along the mossy wall on their own eternal quest. Their brave companion who was somewhere soaring free in a sky of love, knew just as they did that one day they would all meet yet again, to explore together wingtip-to-wingtip. I walked back home to laugh and cry with Mom and Dad and tell them about the ravens. —V.C.

— Raven Facts

Ravens know at least 25 vocabulary sounds and often gather to communicate in large social gatherings. They verbalize in croaks, growls, coos, caws, gurgles, screams, screeches, and even rattles. Not only does each whole flock have a common call, but each individual raven has a unique identifying call as well. There are many reports of demonstrations of the intelligence of ravens, including how they have learned to use railroad tracks as a way of breaking open their food. They just put the bag, can, or nut on the tracks and when the train comes by, voila! Fast food!

Salmon

The Vision Keeper

If Salmon has chosen to appear to you, it is asking you to encourage that part of yourself that believes in a vision with a single-minded passion.

almon spirit is the focused willpower to go after a dream, to whole-heartedly invest in a potential. It pursues its goal determinedly, persevering no matter how difficult to achieve or far away it may seem. It believes that success comes by taking the long journey in small daily increments. Salmon's resolve is such that all alone it will fight the opposing currents, even though there may be no verifiable evidence that its vision can be achieved. Encountering Salmon spirit means that you must now rededicate yourself with passion to manifesting your dream!

BEWARE of losing your connection with the source and becoming unbalanced on a journey of self-gratification.

The Fish Who Wouldn't Leave

T WAS A HOT summer day. I was wading in the shallow waves, out on a sand bar, admiring the patterns in the sand. All around me were children playing, surfers on their boards riding the waves, athletic couples playing water Frisbee and teenagers whooping loudly while they body-surfed. I was contemplating braving the large breakers and going out beyond them to swim. But I felt content just to stand quietly and watch all the action.

Suddenly, swimming between my feet was a large fish, which I later realized was a salmon. Instead of swimming away, he just stayed quietly between my legs, as if resting. I laughed and talked to him and told him to go back out to sea where he would be safe. Because he did not move away, I reached underwater and gently guided him back out to the deeper water and launched him in the right direction. Several people nearby were watching me in amazement. I returned to my wading spot, shaking my head. I had barely turned around, when there he was again! Now I was the one who was amazed! Here, with so many other pairs of legs to choose from, he had found me again!

"Is that your pet fish?" the man next to me asked. PET FISH? I could tell from the man's expression that he was half-serious. I also thought it was somewhat odd, but not that odd. After all, I had saved many fish in my life, and maybe this one needed my help. I always expect the unusual and it usually finds me—even if it is a fish. So here I was, with this friendly fish, again.

This time, determined to succeed, I swam him out past the medium-size waves and gave him a big push. He calmly looked at me and then followed me back in. This was too much! What was the right thing to do here? Perhaps he was disoriented and couldn't get past the huge breakers. Salmon or no salmon, I didn't blame him, as they were very intimidating. So, there was nothing else to do. I was definitely going swimming, and with a friend. Taking a deep breath, somehow I managed to get myself and the fish out past the breakers by timing it just right. This time, without looking back, he swam away, out to sea. I treaded water for a minute to see if he would return, half hoping he would.

Suddenly, careening right over my head and swooping down like a dive-bomber came a large seagull. He hit the water with a splash and scooped up "my" salmon and took off with it wriggling wildly in his mouth. I shouted up angrily at the seagull as he happily flew off with the wildly flapping fish. There was absolutely nothing I could do. I was shocked. With a heavy heart weighing me down, I swam back to shore. I lay down on my blanket, heartbroken over a brief but magical relationship with a salmon. There wasn't anyone I could tell who would understand. I hid my face in my arms. Even though the whole experience had lasted less than ten minutes, I felt like I had just lost a close, dear friend. —V.C.

—Salmon Facts

Salmon travel as much as 10,000 miles, eluding predators of all kinds, including eagles, bears, whales, sharks, seals, porpoises and fishermen, not to mention the perils of pollution and development of their spawning ground, to return to the very same stream of their birth. How do salmon know the way back to their native birthplace? It is part of the mystery of salmon. Scientists believe that they return to the right coastline by sensing both the ocean currents and the earth's magnetic field. When they reach "their" coast, the salmon's strong sense of smell guides them to "their" river and tributary, each having its own unique smell. The salmon then follow it to precisely their original breeding tributary to spawn. Of the 3,000 eggs the female lays in the spawning ground, a mere 300 survive, and of those only four or five reach maturity, with even fewer returning two to three years later to spawn. Considering the hardships of its short life, it is amazing that any salmon survive in the wild at all.

Snake

Flexibility

If Snake has chosen to appear to you, it is asking you to encourage that part of yourself that is willing to bend flexibly to consider new ideas and accept new situations.

nake spirit, while not afraid to rise up for what it believes in, does not rigidly adhere to a single plan. It moves energetically and gracefully into the future to accept new ideas that come with change. Wise Snake spirit easily sheds what it has outgrown and moves forward expansively and fluidly toward a new position. By encountering Snake, consider whether you are resisting new ideas. Try taking on the Snake spirit of flexibility. Loosen up, relax with things as they are. Try not to rigidly make them conform with how you think they must be. Breathe into your life. Go in peace.

REMEMBER to discriminate. If you listen to your heart you will know when to discard what is ready to fall away and when to keep what is valuable.

The Moccasins

S A YOUNG GIRL, I had the rich blessing of growing up in the woods of Connecticut. One of my favorite pastimes was to roam in the woods and find wild and secret places. I would look for wildflowers, hidden woodland streams and wild animals. I looked too for the presence of spirit beings: Native American spirits and forest spirits who I believed were secretly watching me and guiding me.

When I was 16, a friend took me deep into an unexplored woods, showing me an old Indian grave site with many old stone markers spread across a hidden meadow. We were very much drawn to exploring everything Native American and here we had found our own special secret in a nearby woods! We spent a lot of time walking around and around, looking at every stone even though there was no writing of any kind. We sat for a long time, feeling the peaceful, sacred beauty of this place with its mysterious shadowed lighting.

As we turned to leave, I noticed something leaning against one of the grave markers. It was a pair of plain deerskin moccasins, old and used, and just my size! I tried them on and we laughed in amazement. They were a perfect fit. I felt it was a gift to me from the ancestors and I wore them home. I loved those moccasins and especially how they had come to me.

But more and more I felt it was not right for me to have them, that they didn't belong to me. I decided to take them back. So one spring day, all alone and with moccasins in hand, I walked out the long barely discernible path through the woods, hoping I could find the gravesite on my own. I looked over a vine covered stone wall, and there was the meadow, quietly resting in late fall afternoon shadows. I stepped carefully in thoughtful reverence toward the area where I had originally found the moccasins.

Suddenly, I stopped short. There was a loud whooshing sound, just like the sound you might expect a soul to make if it were escaping from under its grave! Heart racing, I backed up quickly. Silence. I took a deep breath and tried cautiously approaching the site from another direction. Again, and even louder—a whooshing-hissing sound. Now, with adrenaline pumping through my body, knees shaking, I stood absolutely rigid with fright. Never mind putting the moccasins back on the site where I had found them, they would be just as fine left right where I stood!

I was thinking seriously about the idea of running when I heard a slight noise and, looking harder, I gasped as I saw a large snake slipping out of a hole in front of

the very grave marker that I had just been approaching. After pausing to look at me intently, the snake headed off, winding through the graveyard and moving away into the woods. I let out a huge laugh! Was I ever relieved! Not an escaping soul out to punish me for taking the moccasins, but thankfully, an all too earthly protective snake. After watching the snake disappear into the woods, I bent down and left the old moccasins by the grave stone next to his hole. I said a blessing and turned to leave as the dark fall air grew cold in the shadowed graveyard. After climbing over the crumbling stone wall, I turned in the path to look back at the moccasins. I smiled. I knew they were back in their rightful place. It was my gift brought back to this secret sacred spot and to the guardian snake spirit who protected it. I turned and walked down the old unused path in the woods toward home, singing. —V.C.

— Snake Facts

Snakes are a part of the reptile (from the Latin repere meaning "crawling") family. Snake bodies contain heart, lungs, stomach and other organs which, just like their bodies, are long and narrow. Without legs or fins, how do snakes move? In an average-sized snake there are more than 100 spinal vertebrae, (as compared to only 33 in a human) which gives it flexibility in bending and coiling. Snakes have six common methods of movement: undulating in an "s" shaped path, side winding, accordion folding and bunching, swimming, gliding from tree to tree, and slithering by moving its belly shutes. The fastest snakes can move as quickly as five miles per hour for a brief time.

Spider

Creating Your Own Path

If Spider has chosen to appear to you, it is asking you to encourage that part of yourself that holds all that you require to achieve your inherent potential.

Spider spirit endlessly weaves its own pattern of creative expression, never running out of new designs. It is endowed with a genius for perpetual creation, building its own secure path of beauty. Spider mother creates the circle-web of all life in which everything that exists is strongly inter-connected. Spider's web creation catches even the smallest plain dew drops of dawn reflected as rainbow jewels. Encountering Spider spirit prompts you to feel your oneness with all your relations and the equality of all beings floating interwoven in the universal web. Realize that your unique part is necessary to complete the diversity of the Creator's web of life.

REMEMBER that gifts renew themselves best when given away freely to inspire others.

A Bathroom Companion

ACH MORNING AS I brushed my teeth, I would peer sleepily into the antique mirror that hung above the sink. One day while fumbling for the soap to wash my face, I reached down to the scallop shell that held the soap and stopped short. There in a large gauzy web that swung from the shell up to the toothbrush holder was perched a delicate spider with long willowy legs. As I picked up the soap, he scurried away and hid behind the sink. I admired his overnight handiwork—a "hammock" web—and continued with my morning preparations.

That evening, upon returning to the bathroom, I looked for him. He was in his web. I talked to him and reached out one finger toward him very slowly. Again he scurried away. I named him Atticus and instructed my boys not to bother him or the web. I was already attached to him. Every morning and evening thereafter, I reached out to touch him, talking to him. I noticed that each day he became bolder and bolder, no longer leaving when I reached toward him. On the fourth day, as I reached out for him as usual, he raised up one of his long fragile legs and waved it toward my finger. I slowly reached out and we touched! I don't know which of us was more surprised. Thereafter, every day we greeted each other this way.

Often when I would appear, he would move to the edge of the web nearest me, and wave one leg in my direction, reaching out to touch, before I did. Sometimes I would go into the bathroom just to say hello! No one would believe me if I said that I had a spider for a friend, so I kept it to myself. Sometimes while brushing my hair, one long hair would fall into his web. Atticus would scurry over, checking it out to see if it was alive. He would then very carefully extract it and let it fall. He liked a tidy web! I suspect he was looking up at me in reproach. He seemed to have such a big personality for such a tiny individual. I could not get Charlotte from Charlotte's Web out of my mind. Would Atticus one day leave a message for me woven in his web? And what would it say? "Don't forget to floss?"

One morning a few weeks later, my little friend was not in his web or anywhere else I looked in the bathroom. I was heartbroken. As I cleaned up the tired dusty web, I thought that brushing my teeth would now return to being its regular, uneventful, boring experience. I would no longer be able to look at spiders in the same way, thanks to Atticus, who taught me that friendships come in all sizes. —V.C.

—Spider Facts

Most people think of spider webs as the beautiful, symmetrical orb web with its spiraling design, but there are many, many different designs which spiders build. Some are as simple as a single sticky strand; others are as complex as suspended hammocks, domes, and sheets. The orb web is extremely efficient. With only a small outlay of silk, it forms a strong and flexible structure in which to trap flying insects. Some spiders weave shining white silk zigzag bands which serve to advertise the web's presence so that birds don't accidentally fly through and destroy it. When the damage to a web is too great, spiders recycle their old silk by eating it to gain much needed protein.

Turtle

The Power of Patience

If Turtle has chosen to appear to you, it is asking you to encourage that part of yourself that is patient and content in non-action, secure in the rightfulness of what is.

Turtle quietly considers all possibilities before moving thoughtfully in its own chosen time. It is never pushed into action by the frantic pace of the restless world. It makes its own decisions from inner strength, waiting in stillness for guidance. It contemplates a spacious awareness, a right action, a right relationship with others and its environment. Often the most correct action is in stillness, listening to the quietness of now. Turtle does not pursue illusive dreams, but values most a focused mind, a patient approach with an honest, candid, guileless attitude. By encountering Turtle spirit, you now act from the fullness of patience and are not motivated by the weak energy of fear to act impulsively.

BEWARE of moving so cautiously that you never dare to extend yourself or try something new and innovative.

The Old Turtle

EARS AGO ON A trip to the Caribbean, I went "atoll hopping" in a rented sailfish. A sailfish is a tiny boat, basically a surfboard with a large sail that skims very fast on the tops of waves across the ocean. It was a beautiful day for island-hopping, and sailing from one tiny deserted island to another, I explored coral reefs and empty white sandy atolls.

I was cutting through the turquoise waves when suddenly a large fish with a long pointed spear for a nose went flying by me in the air! He was going in the same direction, yet even faster than I. He hit the water ahead of me with a large splash and then again launched himself majestically way up into the air. He did this over and over. I was amazed but then I saw why. An extremely large dark sleek shape—not much smaller than my boat—was fiercely chasing him, right on his tail. Was it a shark? The little swordfish was running for its life! I was immediately drawn into the drama and my heart raced wildly. I headed my little boat to follow the fleeing swordfish. Was there any way I could help?

Suddenly, to my horror, the swordfish took one long last flying leap through the air, only to land with a heavy thud on the beach of an atoll just ahead. I hauled on the sail to increase my speed and headed straight for the atoll at a brisk run. I too, beached the boat with a hard thud and was immediately on the run toward the fish. I had to be very wary of the many large black pointed spines of sea urchins that were everywhere amidst the rocks in the shallow water. I sprinted up to the fish, who, lying on his side, was breathing heavily and eyeing me with increasing panic. I knew I had to act fast. Running down to the water I wet my hands and arms and raced back to the fish. Gently I scooped him up and hurried back to the water's edge. Carefully I laid him down in the shallow blue-green water. At first he moved sluggishly. Was I too late? Then he started wiggling and wiggling and finally with a large splash of his tail, he swam away, apparently fully recovered!

I was so caught up in the thrill of the encounter that I was greatly startled to hear something move nearby. I even thought I heard a small cough. As far as I knew the atoll was deserted. I swung around and there, lying in the white sand, staring at me with large sand-encrusted eyes, was the largest sea turtle I had ever seen. He looked very old and not at all afraid of me. He seemed more mystical than real. I half expected him to speak. Was he the guardian spirit of the sea, come to thank me for saving the life of the swordfish? Or would he perhaps scold me for upsetting the balance of the natural world, stepping in where I didn't belong?

At that moment I didn't care if I did "upset the balance." I had saved the flying fish and I was glad for it. I did belong here too, didn't I? The old turtle sat silently, unmoving, watching me with sad and wise grandfather-eyes. Had he come up here on the sand to die? I knew I had no special abilities that could save him as I had saved the fish. I sat quietly, honoring his beauty. After a while it seemed right for me to go and quietly leave him alone on his island. I sailed away feeling an unspoken friendship, looking back over my shoulder at the turtle, waving good-bye again and again until I could no longer see him.

Why did I feel like crying? What was it that had just happened? What did it all mean? A young woman under the watchful gaze of an old sea turtle had saved the life of a flying fish with a sword for a nose. The lives of three separate beings who had never known each other before were mysteriously woven together by the Creator for a brief moment in eternity, on a deserted island floating in a beautiful turquoise blue sea. —V.C.

—Turtle Facts

Giant loggerhead sea turtles are the most common marine turtles in North American waters. They have been crawling from the sea to lay their eggs on the shore for millions of years. Recently, though, man's activities in their hatching sites has severely threatened them. Now only a small percentage of hatchlings survive to maturity, due to such problems as free roaming pets, pollution (such as floating plastic bags, fast food foam and other non-biodegradable materials); and lighted beaches (which cause the hatchlings to go in the opposite direction of the ocean). Loss of nesting habitats and drowning in shrimp and fishing nets have also caused a devastating decline to these and other sea turtles.

Whale

The Collective Consciousness

If Whale has chosen to appear to you, it is asking you to encourage that part of yourself that lives in communion with the universal community.

hale spirit, rather than being a single self-conscious instrument, immerses itself within the symphony of life, in the deepest waters of the collective consciousness. It understands that everything we do individually affects the collective health and well-being of each of us on the planet. Whale listens more carefully to the blending of many songs than to the single song of a particular individual. Whale is your greater self coming to remind you to put your small self aside, and to remember your larger purpose of serving the whole. Encountering the great-hearted Whale, you look away from the illusion that we are each separate from one another, and choose the consciousness of planetary cooperation to effect integration throughout the entire community of Earth.

REMEMBER that the most powerful, life-enhancing ideas are those that advance all species equally.

The Eye of Love

HAVE HAD MANY encounters with whales, having lived on three islands in three different corners of the U.S. But one day while out on a small whale watching boat in the Pacific Ocean I had a life changing experience that affirmed for me the power of inter-species communication. From a safe distance I was watching a magnificent herd of Gray Whales and saw some spectacular whale displays. Then the captain announced that it was time to say good-bye and head back to port. He turned his ship and all the whale watchers left the deck to go inside as it was bitter cold and extremely windy. I, alone, stayed out on the deck straining to see any last sight of the whales that I could. My face was covered in tears as I had been so greatly moved by my encounter with these breath-taking creatures and I had not yet seen enough to fill my soul. Instead of searching the horizon, I closed my eyes and went deep into my heart. I called out to the whales with all my being and thanked them for existing on Earth and for surviving the horrors of what humankind had done to their "tribe". I asked for forgiveness and spoke out my great love for their species.

My eyes popped open when the captain began excitedly shouting on the loud-speaker for all the passengers to "HOLD ON TIGHT TO SOMETHING!" And "WATCH OUT!" I looked down to see the most tremendous gray form headed right for our boat at full speed! I knew exactly what it was and began shouting to it and waving my arms in joy. Right under me she came—with only a few feet of clearance from the bottom of the ship, which now seemed to be such a tiny, tiny boat! I looked down, and right beneath me the whale's huge eye was looking up at me, perhaps only ten feet below. I could see every barnacle and scar on her body. For a brief instant, she and I had a very personal connection.

Later the captain told me that in all his years on the sea, nothing like that had ever happened to him. I will never forget the immense love I saw in that big eye looking up at me. I remember in the moment thinking that that was what I imagined the eye of God to look like. So much love. I knew the great-hearted whale had come to me on the power of a prayer, to complete a circle of love. —V.C.

—Whale Facts

Whales have many qualities in common with humans, among them the ability to communicate. Many species of whales, such as humpback, beluga, narwhals, orcas, and sperm whales have a variety of sounds that have been recorded by scientists. Some of the more simple sounds are clicks, chirps, moos, mews, croaks, burps, whistles, shrills, and screams. Some are complex sounds, repeating sequences of increasingly complicated tonal sounds that appear to be very much like haunting songs. Whales have even been known to mimic the exact tonal patterns that researchers project to them under water. Whales may use sounds in mating rituals, sonar location (echolocation), acoustical mapping, pod communication, or just for the pure joy of "singing." Some whales have distinctive patterns of clicks called codas, or special songs that are unique to either single individuals or to whole collective pods (families that live and travel together), that are believed to be a form of inter-pod identification. Maybe they just do it for pure pleasure—a symphony of whales.

Wolf

Integrity to Self, Loyalty to Family, Commitment to Community

If Wolf has chosen to appear to you, it is asking you to encourage that part of yourself that uses loyalty to create an ennobled life of intention.

Wolf spirit balances family loyalty with the firm resolve to maintain a personal vision. By boldly pursuing its unique vision, Wolf is ultimately able to honor its commitment to the larger community. At the same time, to achieve its personal goals, Wolf spirit must depend above all else upon teamwork within the family and community. By encountering Wolf you are now challenged to run a narrow path, balancing the respectfulness required by relationships with the boldness of your personal quest. Once committed, Wolf never betrays its loyalties or its intentions.

REMEMBER that breaking a covenant destroys not only your integrity, but weakens the family structure as well as the entire fabric of your community.

The Curious Wolf

 HAVE HAD THE GOOD fortune to work with wolves either directly or indirectly, spending thousands of hours "howling" for wolves in various parts of the world. As a wildlife biologist for almost forty years, I have gone out countless times alone into the night to "talk to the wolves." Finding wolves in order to get started usually took a couple weeks of searching. I would hike mile after mile alone at night, stopping every twenty minutes or so to howl. Sometimes loons or frogs would answer me back. Occasionally a black bear would huff in the bushes, or a beaver would slap its tail. While any answer was exciting, the real thrill was to hear the distant mournful song of a wolf pack. During the puppy rearing summer months, I would tent nearby. As the adults came and went, I learned to know who was home tonight and who wasn't, based on their howls. Sometimes they sang on their own. More often they responded to my howl. Being linked to them through sound was a unique experience. They taught me so much.

Usually I did not see them. My goal as a biologist was to learn about them while disturbing them as little as possible. On one occasion, I "called" in the afternoon and a wolf responded. *He then used my howls to track me.* Rarely do wolves come to find out who the "stranger" is. Yet this particular wolf was just too curious; he had to know who this strange loner wolf might be who had called. Imagine his surprise when he finally came upon the source—a howling human!

My fondest memory was of the first wolf that I ever saw. I had been howling to a distant pack, unaware that a wolf was in my immediate presence. In the midst of my calling this impressively long-legged, sleek-coated animal stepped out and looked at me. Our eyes met. After what seemed a few minutes, it turned and loped away, seemingly unconcerned. I was thrilled by the surprise encounter.

Once my assistant, Dave, and I had been out all night "talking" to the wolves. At dawn we got into our canoe, and tied it broadside to some shoreline bushes that hung out over the water. We were both hunched over, feeling very tired. All of a sudden, Dave sat up straight as a wolf poked its nose out of the bushes in front of him. This was Dave's first wolf encounter. He whispered, "What should I do?" I urged him to remain absolutely still. Unwilling to actually touch the canoe, the wolf withdrew and began to move back and forth, peering over the bushes from time to time to look at us. A second wolf joined it. Both whimpered numerous times. Occasionally one or the other would growl a little bit. I doubt that they could figure out what we were, beyond appearing as two blobs in a floating "log." They couldn't detect our scent because it was being drawn out into the middle of the lake where the early morning sun was causing a mist to rise. One of the wolves approached from behind me, walking out into the lake to a depth that little more than covered its paws, all the while waving its nose back and forth. Failing to catch our scent, and unwilling to approach right up to the canoe, it returned to the shore. The wolves left after about twenty minutes. We were sad to see them go. I had waited my entire life for an experience such as this— to be able to observe a wild wolf so distinctly, to be up close enough to touch, to hear and sense every feeling between us as brothers of the forest.

Many seasons will come and go, yet as long as I live I shall never forget these experiences. They enhanced all my life work, while also intensely filling my heart. Long after I am gone, may the wild wolf roam in the forests and on the plains of the Earth. —Paul Joslin.

Dr. Paul Joslin is wildlife biologist of large predators. He has studied wolves and other large carnivores in several countries for nearly forty years. He helped pioneer some of the early understanding of the ecology and behavior of wolves in the field. Currently he is the executive director of the Alaska Wildlife Alliance, www.akwildlife.org, based in Anchorage.

— Wolf Facts

Humans and wolves are the most widely distributed land mammals on earth, having interacted for thousands of years. Wolves once roamed from Florida to Washington and from Mexico to northern Canada. Yet, due to humans, wolves became one of the most oppressed species in North America. Prior to 1960, the wolf was viewed as destructive and evil and was hunted to near extinction. They were killed by the hundreds of thousands. By 1950, 19 of every 20 wolves were exterminated. In the last 40 years the wolves have had a modest comeback, increasing to a population of 70,000, mainly in Canada and Alaska. Presently they are expanding well into Minnesota, Wisconsin, Michigan and Montana, with small populations in Wyoming, Idaho, North Carolina, North Dakota, and Washington. In 1995 re-introduction began of the gray wolf into northern U.S. and the red wolf into the southwest, their native territories. The re-introduction campaigns have proved only somewhat successful, due to ranchers in some states killing off the new arrivals. The wolf has become a popular symbol of the wild and the need for ecological balance.

Calling Animals To You

"It's a different kind of world to grow up in when you're out in the forest with the little chipmunks and the great owls. All these things are around you as presences, representing forces and powers and magical possibilities of life that are not yours and yet are all part of life, and that opens it out to you. Then you find it echoing in yourself, because you are nature."

—Joseph Campbell, The Power of the Myth

ANY PEOPLE HAVE THE gift of being able to draw animals to them, even wild animals. You might have noticed someone who is continually aware of the hidden presence of animals in the wild, or someone who has many special encounters with animals or birds, more than anyone else you know. Why is he or she always the one that sees the animal hiding in the underbrush or camouflaged in the sand or flying far overhead? Perhaps it is because they are "tuned in" to a different frequency—a frequency in which animals communicate. Seeing oneself, not as separate from the whole, but as a piece of the "creation puzzle" allows a human to enter into a new dimension where a universal common code is available. The prerequisite to inter-species communication is the language of the heart, rather than thoughts, which are the language of the mind. By opening your heart all the way, as with someone or something that you dearly love, you attune yourself to a frequency of the heart on which an animal can find you.

As a young mother living in a beachside apartment in Southern California, I would go out very early to the beach to meditate on the sand, by the quiet ocean. I became aware that there was a pod of dolphins that lived along my section of the coast. Sometimes, after finishing a peaceful meditation, I would open my eyes to see dolphins body-surfing in the waves right near me. As each wave curled up in turquoise light, I could see the sleek shiny forms of several dolphins cutting sideways in the breaking wave as if to entertain me. I could almost hear them saying "Look at me! Watch this!" It always filled me with joy to see their grace and beauty.

At that time, my work required me to commute once a week to a large city 100 miles away. The first part of the trip was a lovely drive along the scenic coastal highway. Many times I would stop and park my car off the highway and, although dressed in business clothes, I would carefully crawl out onto the rock walls at the edge of the ocean. Though I was many miles away from my "meditation beach," I would close my eyes and intently "call in" my special pod, believing with all my heart that they would come. I knew that because love knows no time or distance they would "hear" me. Inevitably, each time, after waiting usually for less than five minutes, they would show up, streaking through the waves like shiny gray bullets. Leaping in the air in front of me in apparent greeting they would shout, "Here we are! Here we are!"—at least I liked to think so. I would wave and shout back to them and then, with a full heart, be on my way.

I never told anyone about the dolphins. I kept it our secret, because I strongly believe that animals should remain wild and free and not be used for frivolous pleasure. To me, this personal connection with the dolphins felt like a gift directly from the Creator, an affirmation of the power of love, reminding me to trust in the natural rhythms of the universe.

Sometimes being able to get in contact with an animal may be useful as well. One day upon entering a small restaurant, I noticed that most of the staff and many of the diners were highly agitated. A small finch had mistakenly entered the restaurant and try as hard as everyone could, the bird eluded capture. It fluttered frantically about, in total panic, even landing on the food and on people's heads. I asked everyone to stop shouting, be calm and stay still. Then, going deep within my heart, I "called" to the bird, within the stillness that comes from honoring it. Letting the compassion in my heart guide me, not my logical mind, I tuned in to what the bird was feeling. I became the bird's feelings. I saw myself in a relationship dimension, as already having merged with the bird. Then, approaching it with the quickness of a bird vibration, I took hold of it in my hands. After talking quietly to it and stroking it gently, I set it free outside, to the applause of the staff and diners.

To call animals to you, first start practicing an acute sensitivity to them. All of creation exists within a particular pattern of energy, each species having its own unique quality or frequency. An animal's particular psychic energy creates a template for their behavior. A turtle has a very slow, calm, inward vibration while a hummingbird has a very fast, energetic, outward energy. The playful, intimate energy of a dolphin is quite different from the noble, aloof energy of a wolf. Communication with wild animals does not occur in the physical dimension, through gestures or words, but in the psychic dimension. Spirit Animals are located in a dimension of symbiotic relationships, in which beings with harmonious consciousness easily find their complement and join together. In this realm of intuitive knowledge, the answer you are seeking is busy seeking you to complete (complement) itself. On this spiritual landscape there are endlessly evolving relationships of reciprocal respect and integration with no limiting personal boundaries.

"Calling" must done from an open, appreciative heart, never from an opinionated, self-oriented mind. The mind is impatient and restless, too certain of how things should be to see the unexpected: the tiny newt hidden like a jewel under the leaf; the rusty fox peering from behind the lichened rock, the cougar track in the damp sand. The key is to remain open to the spontaneous nature of the gift, which will rarely fit your expectations or goals. To call successfully, one must have a humble attitude of seeker requesting guidance, not a superior stance as the "most evolved, most significant" species. Concentrate on the unique qualities that you most admire about that creature and silently express all of your appreciation for its existence. Gratitude and appreciation create openings in the veil that normally hide wildlife from humans.

With a heightened sensitivity to the animal's frequency pattern, an understanding of where they are vibrationally located, and an open, appreciative and humble heart, you are prepared to "call." Most importantly, you are able to be heard. Release your connection to your own human energy field and slip deeply into your heart. Immerse yourself into the mystical vibratory current, the qualities of the animal you are seeking. Over and over, in the deepness of your heart, call for that animal, asking for guidance, asking to become a more perfect part of all that is. By practicing this exercise frequently, with a passionate belief and a heart filled with love, you will enter into a realm of gifted relationships with endless possibilities.

Calling is being willing to share an open space of exploration with another species that allows the spontaneous, the awesome, even the sacred to appear. It is an extraordinary realm that co-exists inside of the ordinary. Once the nature explorer experiences this dimension of intuition, they are forever transformed, never to be the same "separate" individual again. One is left hungering for a deeper intimacy and further dialog with the whole Earth community— an extraordinary realm that uses the universal heart to hear messages of new possibilities .

Spirit Animals are urgently calling out: "Do you see us? Do you hear us? Look for us, listen for us, reach for us—we are here! We are waiting for you to remember our ancient bonds of community, to honor us, your relatives, with care for the Earth and the wellbeing of us all. We are waiting for you to remember yourselves and to cherish one another. We are waiting and we are watching. Please—look for us—and remember."

When an animal brings you the blessing of a message and you receive it, you are strengthening the woven bonds of creation, and are obliged to honor their gift by extending one of your own. Your "blessing returned" might be a quiet thank you, a prayer, an affirmation, or a wish for that animal's protection. The relationship is fortified by your ceremonial act of offering back the gift of a flower, a rock, or a feather laid in the place where you were honored. All of this must be done and said in silence and always from the heart, for it is the heart that holds the common vision.

By a reciprocal honoring in this way, blessing will be placed upon blessing, like stone upon stone. You now anchor the animal, the message, the learning, and yourself into the Earth, where the knowledge of it will lay beneath the ancient rocks, kept for all time. The Earth will remember this blessing long after all of you who took part in it are gone, for patterns of love are never lost. They become an inheritance—a blessingway—that lightens the path for those to come.

Remember the blessingway and walk it in peace.

Your Spirit Animal Guardian

O CHOOSE TO HAVE a spirit animal guardian is a gift that adds power, perception and protection to your life. If you wish to choose a guardian animal, there are many ways to do so. You may already know just which animal it is, through a dream or vivid vision that strongly impressed you, or an encounter in the wild. Perhaps you have always had a deep attraction to a certain species. When the thought of a certain animal "quickens your heart," that animal is choosing you. If you decide to use *Spirit Animals* to help you choose your guardian animal, listen first with all your ability to your inner voice, your intuition. No matter how inexperienced you are with this process, if you make the choice with your heart it will be the right one. Then simply open the book. Your heart will always guide you to open to the right page. The choice may surprise you. Don't expect it to be your favorite animal, or one you would have ever chosen for yourself, but accept it: this is Spirit speaking! The reason for this animal being chosen for you will become apparent later on. It is an honor that you should treasure privately, kept quietly unseen in your heart, not something to talk about with others.

Your guardian animal might change later in your life, and you might have several guardian animals, depending on your need. I have one that I think of as the symbol of my heart, and another that I think of as the reflection of my spirited nature. Recently I had the gift of seeing my two animal guardians encountering each other! As I was watching a stag deer browse in a meadow, to my surprise, a hawk flew down and landed on a rancher's old rotting fence post, just feet away from the deer. They both stopped and stared intently at each other for a long moment and then the deer slowly moved away. I felt so honored to witness them encountering one another. To me it was a meaningful symbol of my heart and spirit speaking to one another, coming into alignment.

I carry a hawk feather in my wallet, to help remind me to become more like the qualities of this animal. I also carry a small deerskin pouch with a deer antler tied to it, with a small piece of deer fur inside, to empower me in times of trouble and weakness. If your spirit animal is a bear or wolf it might be harder to find an actual piece of the animal, but if you call to your animal and ask for it, it will show up later in your life in a mysterious way. It might take a long time, but when you most need it, it will manifest.

Call on your guardian animal whenever you need guidance, empowerment or vision. The message will always appear, written everywhere on the wind. And yet, like the wind, you must first become open. Open to change. Open to experiencing the communion of spirit. Open to the wonder of spontaneous encounters with Spirit Animals.

In wildness is the preservation of the world. — Henry David Thoreau

Cherish the Wildness

E ARE CURRENTLY BETWEEN two and four million species strong on this marvelously rich planet, living in a diverse, organic, symbiotic and vitally thriving relationship with one another. Or is it thriving? We are thought by increasingly more and more biologists to be in the midst of the sixth major global extinction on earth, with approximately 30,000 species being lost a year. Our ecosystems are daily weakening and the basic structure of Earth's ecology is being gravely eroded. This extinction epidemic has been rapidly brought on by a single species: homo sapiens. Due to over-hunting, over-harvesting and over-developing, we are witnessing a critical loss of the vast global diversity in both the plant and animal worlds.

If the biodiversity of life within any particular ecosystem is degraded, with all of its vital local and global functions, it is not long before our species will be critically threatened as well, for we are all deeply related. As Thomas Berry said, "When other living species are violated so extensively, the human itself is imperiled."

To many a modern man, wild animals are competitors, even destructive enemies, or at the very least, inconvenient pests. Our society has destroyed or is presently seeking to destroy whole species, thus actively—yet unknowingly—prompting the next great extinction on earth. Could it be that the underlying reason for the desire to eliminate the wild is that we have become afraid of that which is free and uncontrollable? Wolves, mustangs, mountain lions, coyotes, bears and raptors represent that which is wild and untamed within us. That which we cannot manage, predict or rule with authority, we seek to obliterate from the Earth, or at least from our small private piece of Earth. "Let it live elsewhere." But "elsewhere" is rapidly disappearing into vast fields of cement, rivers of paved roads, and oceans of greed. The wild has been run off newly cultivated lands and placed in confinement, in amusement parks and zoos for the civilized to safely view. As any wildlife biologist can tell you, the animals of the planet are gravely imperiled. We cannot call ourselves naturalists or nature lovers and turn aside from a "nation's" silent cry for help.

Wildness is not just a location. Wildness is an understanding—a landscape of mind—that must be vigilantly cherished if it is to survive. If we are to save our native species and our natural space, we need to act passionately and decisively. For the spiritual naturalist, the survival of our planet is no longer just an issue of caring or a desire for beauty. It has become an urgent crisis, requiring a focused life and a radical resolve that actively seeks to promote and protect the sustainability of our precious planet.

Many naturalists and biologists have become greatly alarmed at the serious decline of amphibians in North America, which are considered by many to be the "barometer" of a healthy ecosystem. One of many theories for the decline is that the amphibians' fragile eggs are being damaged by increased exposure to ultra-violet rays through a weakened protective ozone layer. In some areas of North America, certain amphibians have already disappeared.

How can one grasp the unknown value of that which is passing away, never to be regained? As a child I grew up being lulled to sleep on hot summer nights by a loud chorus from the pond of bullfrogs, spring "peepers" and tree toads. My heart aches with the possibility of the extinction of my precious bullfrogs. They are my childhood tribe—I am bound up with these "frog people," a part of my personal mythology. From the red-winged blackbird calling from his marsh perch, to the bright beady-eyed raccoon with her delicate, graceful paws, all the birds and small creatures of the woodlands make up the mosaic pattern of my childhood.

Some say it is too late to reverse the sixth extinction. Yet I believe that it is never too late. It is simply time for every one of us—in every generation, from the children to the elders—to act. We must all speak out loudly and take daily actions, no matter how small, both locally and globally to protect the biodiversity of our planet. To protect its valuable, wild inhabitants; the habitats they live in, and the systems they not only depend on, but help to create. The giant loggerhead sea turtle gliding through the turquoise waters and the red-tailed hawk gliding through the currents of the air, cannot speak out in their defense. It is up to us—the very species who has threatened life for us all—to create healing on the planet, a goal that is still possible to achieve. It is my prayer that our grandchildren and their grandchildren will be able to roam the forests free and wild as I did, peering at the astonishing faces of salamanders, into the open eyes of owls and down the velvet throats of "jack-in-the-pulpits," that they too, may have the privilege of searching the natural world for the mysteries of life, and find them reflected, as I did, deep within their own heart.

The essential formations of nature pronounce Love at each turn of the path. Yet it is a path that many of us have walked with eyes and ears and hearts closed. The trees, plants, animals, minute insects and vast systems of Earth are calling to us to join with them in a celebration dance of spirit. When we bring ourselves merely up to the perimeter of the circle of the dance, as spectators, we only half see our purpose on Earth. Yet when we bring our whole selves and our whole heart, stepping into the circle to join the dance, taking the hands and wings and paws and fins and claws of our brothers and sisters, we help to spin the web of creation into balance. By joining the honoring, we become very simply, the celebration of Spirit itself.

All of nature is watching us now, to see what we, the humans will do. What choices, what sacrifices, what commitments shall the humans make? The question now is, will we at the last moment remember ourselves and become a part of all that is? Or will we stay, poised uncertainly, on the edge of experience, failing to engage with the Earth's great potential? And if by failing to take our proper place the whale and the wood thrush fade away, who then will sing into the wind and the water, the brilliant melodies of Earth?

It is our misfortune that for most of us that clear-eyed vision, that true instinct for what is beautiful and awe-inspiring, is dimmed and even lost before we reach adulthood. If I had influence with the good fairy who is supposed to preside over the christening of all children I would ask that her gift to each child in the world be a sense of wonder so indestructible that it would last throughout life, as an unfailing anti-dote against the boredom and disen-chantments of later years, the sterile preoccupation with things that are artificial, the alien-ation from the sources of our strength.

—*Rachel Carson*

ON THE TRAIL

N THE QUIET, seemingly empty woods, we stop briefly on the trail. Yet we do not stand alone. There are others of great heart present nearby, yet hidden from us, in a wild world from which they silently watch us pass. If only when we pause, we would reach out with honor to call to them. Hearing, they would answer, for they know us. Here in the cool forest, on the ocean shore, in the river canyon, on the starlit desert, from every corner of the Earth, they appear, to guide us home. We turn now, eyes finally open, aware of whom we meet: Spirit Animals! Stopping briefly on the trail, we do not stand alone.

Victoria Covell grew up roaming the woods and seashore of Connecticut, looking for the hidden mystical—both forest fairies and mythical mermaids. She has lived in wild places in all four corners of the United States as well as in the Rocky Mountains of Colorado. Presently, she lives in a log cabin with her two sons, Noah and Seth, in the forest of the Sierra Nevada Mountains. One of her favorite pastimes is peering into a microscope at micro flora and fauna-the littlest "Spirit Animals" of the planet.

Noah Buchanan has always had a deep interest in the symbolic, mythic and heroic found in art and nature. He studied classical drawing and painting at the Pennsylvania Academy of Fine Arts, the nation's oldest art school. He graduated from the University of California at Santa Cruz and is pursuing a Masters degree at the New York Academy of Art in New York City. Noah has also illustrated the award-winning book *Places of Power* (Dawn Publications). He joyously collaborated with the author—his mother—on this book.

Other Distinguished Nature Awareness Books from Dawn Publications

With Beauty Before Me, by Joseph Cornell, is a pocket-sized gem perfect for nature walks. With its inspiring quotations and introspective nature exercises, it can lead you to new heights of serenity and a sense of oneness with Mother Nature.

Listening to Nature, by Joseph Cornell, is a journey into the essence of nature, with stunning photographs and Cornell's irrepressible enthusiasm. It offers meditative and dynamic ways for adults to achieve peace through nature.

Sharing Nature with Children (vols. I & II), by Joseph Cornell. These classic nature awareness guidebooks are a treasury of nature games for parents, teachers, scout leaders, or anyone wanting to help children to appreciate nature.

Play Lightly on the Earth, by Jacqueline Horsfall, is written especially with 3 to 9 year olds in mind, and packed with original activities with an emphasis on creative thinking, problem-solving, and skill development—all in the guise of play.

Nature Awareness Books for Children

Places of Power, by Michael DeMunn, reveals the places that native people all over the world have always known have natural power, and explores with children how to become attuned to their own places of power.

Wonderful Nature, Wonderful You, by Karin Ireland, shows how nature can be a great teacher, reminding us to do things at our own pace and to bloom where we are planted.

Do Animals Have Feelings Too? by David L. Rice, is an illustrated collection of true observations of animal behaviors, both heart-warming and thought-provoking, showing the variety of animal feelings.

When God Made the Tree, by Virginia Kroll, shows trees, animals and people forever linked in an intimate relationship that suggests the greatness of their Creator.

Little Brother Moose, by James Kasperson, is based on the tendency of moose to wander into towns. This moose gets lost in urban adventures, but finds his way home by listening with his whole being.

Dawn Publications is dedicated to inspiring a deeper understanding and appreciation for all life on Earth. To order, or for a copy of our catalog, please call 800-545-7475, or visit our web site at www.dawnpub.com.